About the Author

Peter Feuerherd is the editor of *American Catholic* and a widely respected Catholic journalist. A former news editor at *The Long Island Catholic* and national affairs writer at the *National Catholic Register*, Feuerherd holds a bachelor's degree in theology and history from St. John's University, New York, and a master's degree in political communications from State University of New York, Albany; he currently serving as communications consultant for the New York Province of the Jesuits. His work has appeared in *New York Newsday*, *Religion News Service*, *Catholic News Service*, the *National Catholic Reporter*, *Commonweal* (including one cover feature), the *German Catholic News Agency*, *The Tablet* (London), and *St. Anthony Messenger*.

Holy Land USA

A Catholic Ride Through America's Evangelical Landscape

PETER FEUERHERD

A Crossroad Book
The Crossroad Publishing Company
New York

The Crossroad Publishing Company
16 Penn Plaza—481 Eighth Avenue, Suite 1550
New York, NY 10001

Printed in the United States of America

The text of this book is set in Sabon
The display faces are Regular Joe and Birch

Library of Congress Cataloging-in-Publication Data is available.

ISBN-10 0-8245-2297-4
ISBN-13: 978-0-8245-2297-1

1 2 3 4 5 6 7 8 9 10   09   08   07   06

Contents

Holy Land, USA

It's late June in Orlando. Not yet noon, and it's already hitting close to 90 degrees. Three dozen or so tourists line up to pay $29.99 per ticket—cheap by Orlando theme park standards—to see the Holy Land, or a reasonable facsimile thereof, near Route 4 in central Florida.

"Are we going on a bunch of rides?" one little boy asks. "Sorry, kid," I think. I have stumbled into a kind of convention of Ned Flanders—the evangelical neighbor of cartoon bumbler Homer Simpson. I was surrounded by shorts and T-shirts proclaiming The Rock, The Lamb—even one that says Read Between the Lines, with a picture of the back of a crucified Christ, complete with stark red blood stripes. When we enter, the sign for the cafeteria advertises Goliath Burgers and Bedouin beef. That little boy isn't in Disney anymore.

This center of evangelical kitsch next to Route 4 is the last place in the world a liberal New Yorker like me would ever imagine being. But I'm here because there's a phenomenon happening in this country, and here is one of the best places to study it.

America used to be considered a Protestant nation, meaning one dominated by old mainline denominations. But their numbers and influence have declined. Other books have traced that decline. My intention is to examine who and what has filled the vacuum they left.

Religiously, in terms of sheer numbers, America has become a country dominated by Catholics (65 million, although many of those are only baptized and haven't darkened a church doorstep in years) and evangelicals (60 million by one estimate, although the definition remains loose). Of course there are other players on the religious scene—practicing secularists, Jews, growing numbers of Muslims, and the historically African American churches—who also incorporate evangelical elements in their prayer and community life. Yet it's still evangelicals and Catholics who largely shape the American religious landscape.

Whenever the issue of religion and politics arises, it's almost always in the context of arguments over whether zealous Catholics and evangelicals have crossed the Maginot Line of America's barrier between church and state. Whenever there's a religious scandal brewing, you can be sure, if it makes the big media, it will involve Catholics or evangelicals. It's the death of a leader of the Catholic world that makes for international television vigils. Few have stayed up late awaiting the funeral of the head of the World Council of Churches. Catholics have the schools and other institutions that sometimes exist uneasily in the midst of a secular society; evangelicals have the zeal to push their vision of a Christocentric world, or at the least their vision of the Gospel.

While these two groups have been left holding the religious vision, there have been, till relatively recently, little contact between the two or, at best, mostly strained relations. Catholic immigrants and their descendants tended to cluster on both coasts and in the industrial Midwest, away from the Bible Belt. And historically, evangelicals looked upon Catholicism as an onslaught of strange and sometimes evil European ways, such as an embrace of alcohol and big-city political machines. It was the evangelical world that fought hardest against Catholic political power in the last two centuries. Opposition to the presidential candidacies of Catholics Al Smith and John F. Kennedy centered on the evangelical community. In 1884, Republicans lost the election when Catholics were offended by a minister at a Republican gathering who castigated the Democrats as the party of "Rum, Romanism, and Rebellion." (Catholics in particular took umbrage at the first two of that trifecta, the last being aimed at the then-Democratic alliance with the old Confederacy.)

"American evangelical Protestants and Roman Catholics have hated one another since the colonial period," sums up William M. Shea, author of *The Lion and the Lamb: Evangelicals and Catholics in America* (Oxford University Press). Those are pretty strong words. But if you examine the history as Shea has, they ring true.

Shea, a professor at St. Louis University, a Jesuit institution, details how strained those relations have been. A 1993 statement titled "Evangelicals and Catholics Together," put together by an informal grouping of scholars from both sides of the divide, was not particularly inspiring, with agreement centered largely on the most generic Christian truths. Yet, notes Shea, the very fact that it was put together at all defied centuries of historical tensions.

Both groups operate on two competing myths, notes Shea. The evangelical movement portrays itself as the heir to the early Christian communities, shorn of Jewish ritual practices, focused on preaching the Word. This was rudely interrupted by the development of a Christian priesthood and hierarchy, challenged only by the re-assertion of the original Christian ideal in the Reformation. Evangelicals see themselves as holding the key to a pristine Church ready to convert the world, always keeping in mind that Jesus is getting ready to return.

On the other hand, Catholics have clung to a belief that Jesus himself established the institutional Church by anointing Peter to be its head. It is an institution more comfortable in history, set for the long term. Rarely do you hear Catholics talk about an imminent return of Jesus. We are trained to encounter history and are proud that we are part of an institution that has lasted 2,000 years. To us, that history give us solace that, even though we know there are sordid times well-documented in our Church, in some mysterious way God has allowed it to continue. In the Catholic vision, Christians are fed by the sacraments, especially the Eucharist, that were established by Jesus and carried on by the early Christians. The Reformation refuted these key doctrines, resulting in confusion and weakness that Christians still suffer from today.

Shea amply documents the bad blood between the two groups in the United States, how these two visions have rubbed raw against each other. As Catholic immigrants attempted to find a foothold in their new country, they were often described as unthinking servants to a foreign master, the pope. Scores of books and Protestant leaders emphasized these points, and they proved central to the anti-Catholic arguments directed at Al Smith and later John Kennedy during their presidential runs. Shea, to be fair, notes that any reading of most pre-Vatican II documents would indicate that the official line of the Church was contrary to many tenets of democracy and independent thought. Throughout the nineteenth century and well into the twentieth, various popes fought the concept that non-Catholic doctrines—or "heresy"—should be allowed to be preached freely. The official Catholic line was that only truth had full rights, and of course, that truth was Catholic truth. Only with Vatican Council II, in the 1960s, did the Church formally embrace the ideas of support for religious freedom articulated by American Jesuit John Courtney Murray and others.

Some of the bad blood lingers on. A pontifical commission on biblical interpretation noted that fundamentalist interpretation of Scripture is a "kind of intellectual suicide." In an address just before becoming pope, Cardinal Joseph Ratzinger (now Pope Benedict XVI) disparaged "sects" who distort the gospel, a term that was widely interpreted as an attack on Latin American evangelicals known for encouraging Catholics to leave the Church.

But those are old battles fought over terrain that is strange to most Americans these days. It almost seems nostalgic to hearken back to those days. We live in a different time. While Smith and Kennedy were castigated for allegedly wanting to impose Catholic rule on the country, Democratic candidate

John Kerry in 2004 was attacked—both by evangelicals and some of his fellow Catholics—for not taking church doctrinal stances on abortion and other issues seriously enough. The old arguments have moved on, and new alliances have been forged.

Today, those worlds of the evangelical and the Catholic are intersecting, playing off each other, influencing how each group adjusts to life in what is often seen as a strange and alien culture. Together, they are seen as inheritors of a Christian vision that embraces a belief in objective reality, even if the attitudes and behaviors of both groups may actually be more complex than advertised.

> Today, evangelical and Catholic worlds are intersecting, influencing how each group adjusts to a strange and alien culture.

Just take a look, for example, at the crowd at the Holy Land in Orlando. A bus delivers a group from a Haitian Pentecostal church. They speak in the French-laden Creole tones of their homeland. They look and talk quite differently from the upper-Midwestern intonations of Ned Flanders. They remind me that evangelicals these days cannot be pigeon-holed into stereotypes of chunky Middle Americans with loud T-shirts. In the same way, American Catholics are as likely to sport surnames like Ruiz and Kim as they are O'Brien or Graziano.

Holy Land itself was developed not by a guy named Billy Bob from Oklahoma or some other Bible Belt outpost. It is the brainchild of Marv Rosenthal, native of Philadelphia, born a Jew, now a proud Hebrew Christian, as they are referred to in some evangelical circles. He started Holy Land after leading some 80 tours to the real Holy Land in the Middle East. Now an ordained minister, he runs Holy Land as a non-profit educational foundation. Marv welcomes close to a quarter of a million believers to his theme park each year.

As I explore Holy Land, I am surprised to discover that it sports elements that can speak to me, a Catholic. The little village square reminds me of my own two trips to the Middle East. Everywhere, biblically based pageants—and, even in some cases, dramas that take liberties with the literal words of the Scriptures—abound. Here there is ample evidence that evangelicals, seen by their affection for Mel Gibson's *The Passion of the Christ*, no longer shy away from visual presentations of the faith. In the last century, evangelical Protestants banned Passion plays in

San Francisco and other American cities. Visual depictions of Christ and other biblical characters were seen as idolatrous. That caution was a relic of the European Reformation wars. I wonder what John Calvin, who ushered in a vision of an austere Christianity focused solely on the Word and bereft of images and icons, would think of Holy Land.

These days, evangelicals like their gospel presented in dramatic style, and the bigger and more flamboyant, the better. And at Holy Land, that's what they get for their $29.99. An actor portraying Jesus—he's friendly but doesn't sign autographs—ambles through the crowd, proclaiming his teachings. Actors portray a woman with a hemorrhage and a blind man who are healed as in the Gospels. Jesus talks up a hard saying about how it's as difficult as a camel—they are grazing in the park—to enter the eye of a needle as it is for a wealthy person to enter the kingdom of God (in the easygoing alliance between suburban-style American affluence and evangelical theology, that is a Gospel passage that is rarely heard among such audiences). Jesus picks up a lamb in his arms and gathers the children in the park around him.

These re-enactments of age-old Christian dramas, often cause for smarmy clichés, work, in their own way. The children are particularly intrigued and the adults pay attention. This Jesus, with bold Semitic features, comes alive. How I wish, I think, that most Catholic liturgical readings could have the vibrancy and drama offered by this Jesus. I've missed Mass this Sunday morning in a strange city, yet I feel that I have received a vivid liturgy of the Word. Not enough to appease that nagging Catholic guilt that tugs at me when I miss Sunday Mass, but it's there nonetheless.

I visit a scaled model replica of ancient Jerusalem. The guide offers us a biblical tour of the city, complete with little toy shepherd boys and Roman soldiers. He concludes his largely scholarly travelogue with an exhortation that Jesus died for everyone and that the key to our existence in this world is "to share our faith." There is no doubt in my mind that a Catholic professor would be content to offer information about ancient Jerusalem and its biblical impact and let it go at that. No evangelical, however, can let a presentation on anything conclude without a pitch for what is described, frequently in code words indecipherable to outsiders, as a call for personal conversion to Jesus.

This regular proselytizing pitch is what disturbs most non-evangelicals about evangelicals. If they could only keep their values to themselves they could be like the Hassidic who live in Brooklyn, or the Amish, a private sect with strict rules of mild curiosity to the rest of the world. But real evangelicals aren't about to hold in their beliefs. It's what makes them who they are.

As Alan Wolfe has noted, American evangelicals will continue to be a force because they believe what this biblical scholar says. They can't help it. Religion is not a private reality. Christianity demands conversion. It's what they believe God calls them to do. "Their whole religious sensibility is based upon meeting the culture halfway," noted Wolfe, a sociologist, in a public television interview in 2004.

Cardinal Avery Dulles, a Jesuit theologian who signed the 1993 document exploring the connections and divisions between evangelicals and Catholics, told me that the clearly articulated way that evangelicals promote such doctrines as the triune God is a strength that other Christians can learn from. "We [as Catholics] can profit from that," he said.

Those strong beliefs, however, can sometimes prove difficult to overcome in formal ecumenical discussions. While the 1993 document passed into the Catholic world with little discussion, it caused a stir among evangelicals. Cardinal Dulles noted that those from the evangelical world who signed the declaration about religious beliefs with Catholics were put on the spot by their co-religionists. Shea notes that the document was a recognition that Catholics are actually Christians as well, a belief that many in the evangelical world were not ready to endorse.

This kind of triumphalism is common in the evangelical world. It can be bewildering to those of us who consider ourselves Christians but haven't experienced the usual evangelical approach to conversion. I remember having a discussion with an evangelical leader who was going off to Ireland to spread Christianity. It was a mission much to my surprise, since I thought St. Patrick had already done the job. But this man told me that few Catholics could earn the Christian label. He felt called to spread the Word in a country where I believed the Word had already been established.

I once attended a meeting of the Evangelical Press Association. At discussions, the word "Christians" was bandied about regularly, and it clearly indicated those who exclusively fit into the evangelical mold. To be honest, as a Catholic, I was insulted. I had had enough when the headline speaker, a prominent evangelical, attempted to explain how the shootings at Columbine High School—big news at the time—were in some ways God's will. They were, he said, a means of illustrating our sinful times. That wrathful god who kills teenagers is rather hard to take to those outside the world of extreme evangelical rhetoric.

Doug Trouten, executive director of the Evangelical Press Association, talked to me from his office at evangelical Northwestern College, where he is associate professor of journalism. Time had healed some of my old wounds from that convention, and Doug, a longtime writer and editor in the evangelical press, was willing to explore with me what makes evangelicals tick and why they sometimes annoy the rest of us.

"The evangelical community makes exclusive truth claims," he says. A community that promotes the biblical injunction that no one can come to the Father but through belief in Jesus is not going to be cozy with what Doug describes as an "I'm OK, You're OK" culture. Easygoing tolerance is not the prime imperative of faithful evangelicals.

But he sees growing cooperation and understanding among Catholics and evangelicals. I tell him about my experience at the evangelical press gathering, and he assures me that the view that Catholics can't be Christians is a distinctly minority one among evangelicals these days.

The barriers are breaking down. He spent decades covering pro-life rallies and demonstrations in the Twin Cities as a reporter and editor with the *Minnesota Christian Chronicle*, a local evangelical newspaper. It is there where perhaps the most common grassroots cooperation and understanding is gradually seeping into the understanding of both camps. Nothing breaks through barriers like a common cause shared on a cold Minnesota morning on a picket line, and

> Nothing breaks through barriers like a common cause shared on a cold Minnesota morning on a picket line.

Doug attests that such alliances have warmed relations between the two groups in the Twin Cities and around the country as well.

Not to say that there aren't differences. Doug is struck by the central place the Scriptures hold in evangelical discourse and culture. On the other hand, Catholics can offer evangelicals a link to Christian tradition, through our repeated prayer rituals that have links to Christians through the ages.

"Our buildings tend to look like shopping malls," says Doug, who expressed admiration for Catholic-style church architecture. Catholic culture, expressed in things such as architecture, links Christian tradition of today with Christians of the past. It is a gift that Catholics bring to American-style Christianity. "Sometimes we think we have to make it all up," he adds, noting the evangelical penchant for spontaneous prayers that, while often heartfelt, lack a sense of historic continuity with Christians who have come and died in the past.

And evangelicals have tended to admire that most Catholic of all symbols, the pope, in particular the late Pope John Paul II. "He was a strong advocate on life and moral issues. He also focused attention on other social issues, caring for the poor and the sick— too often ones that the evangelical community has downplayed." On the day I interviewed Doug, the campus of the evangelical college was adorned with American flags flown at half staff in honor of the recently deceased pope.

When he was growing up, Doug admitted, evangelicals like himself just assumed that Catholics were going to hell. To be fair, the reverse attitude among Catholics about evangelicals was not uncommon, although most Catholics I know rarely entertained the subject. We were often so wrapped up in our own belief system that it was hard to recognize that others existed as well. In the Catholic church I attended growing up on Long Island, I don't think we thought too much about Presbyterians or Methodists.

Not only can evangelicals bring scriptural appreciation to Catholics, but there's also an attitude that Catholics might be well advised to adopt. Doug tells me that the Church's reliance on tradition and culture, while all-embracing and sometimes comfortable, can for many evangelicals get in the way of the important stuff, namely a relationship with Jesus.

Evangelicals see a need for personal conversion in every Christian's life, not simply attending church because one's family always did so. "We are called to be children of God, not grandchildren of God," he says. The phrase is a clever one, and gets me thinking. Doug is onto something. Catholics too often don't address the central issues of faith, have a tendency to fit into the wider culture perhaps too easily—until, of course, life's vicissitudes strike. That may be a central reason why one of the largest Christian groups in the country is former Catholics. (Evangelicals realize, of

17

course, that the seductiveness of American culture and materialism affects them as well.)

There is something else happening to evangelical exclusiveness. While evangelicals are pushing their beliefs upon the culture, the culture is pushing right back. Soon after George Bush was re-elected president in 2004, with scores of media pundits proclaiming that America had fallen sway to the old-time religion, the most popular television show in strong evangelical areas was *Desperate Housewives*, a celebration of soap opera sin reveled in by believers and non-believers alike. The women of Wisteria Lane created must-see Sunday nights all over blue and red America. Their behavior was far from holy, but evangelicals watched as much as anyone else did. "American culture . . . is an enormously powerful force, and it will change religion, just as religion will change culture," concluded Wolfe.

Wolfe, a Jew who teaches at a Jesuit College, has long had an interest in the sociological developments of Middle Americans, including evangelicals. He's come to one conclusion: evangelicals are here to stay, and they will continue to influence the rest of us. At the same time, we will be influencing them.

The obsession with the Great Commission (Mt.

28:16–20) is what sets evangelicals apart. Other Christians, including most Catholics, have learned to live and let live. But true evangelicals cannot let themselves be swayed by an easygoing tolerance of a secular society. They are obsessed with a question central to their belief system, a question most of us find annoying but one that evangelicals relate to as the inquiry that leads to everlasting life. How Christians address that question may point to the divisions that mark relations between Catholics and evangelicals today.

Seeking salvation in all the wrong places

"Are you saved?"
"No," I said . . . "I'm Catholic."

Anna Nussbaum, junior at the University of Notre Dame, describing her encounter with an evangelical worker on a trip to Africa, in an article in *Commonweal*, Dec. 17, 2004

"Are you saved?" This is the one inquiry that divides "us" from "them," literally and figuratively.

Ask that question on any street corner in a major American city, and most people will scamper away as quickly as possible in another direction. For those seeking to win friends and influence people, better to say you have bubonic plague. Whether asked by the sincere religious zealot or the huckster, the question seems to be best ignored.

Yet that question remains perhaps the deepest one a Christian can ask. It deserves an answer, particularly from Catholics and others who are antsy whenever the question is raised.

Perhaps the angst raised by the question is due because it is frequently raised insincerely, as a jumping off point to prove some arcane biblical point or to establish why you should attend one church instead of another. Everyone knows the Bible is a book frequently used as a weapon to prove the point of some dogma. Many of us who are not evangelicals are frankly annoyed by those who feel a need to proselytize.

There was a time when evangelicals rarely ventured out of their world. Some consider that the good old days. That left the rest of us to sit in bemused detachment, never considering that worldview unless a famous preacher was beset with money or sex scandal woes, or there was some dispute in a small town over teaching evolution.

We are no longer so hermetically sealed in our denominational worlds. There is much overlap. Perhaps, if you are a Catholic or mainstream Protestant, you have been confronted at work. Perhaps an evangelical outreach has grabbed a family member, making discussions around the holiday dinner table strained as you reach for the wine goblet and get a strange look from your newly evangelical, and now sober and abstaining, brother-in-law.

Anna Nussbaum is a junior at the University of Notre Dame. A fine writer, she has already published a number of her pieces for *Commonweal*, one of the nation's top journals of religious, social and political opinion.

In a Dec. 17, 2004 piece in *Commonweal*, she describes an encounter with a man aboard a plane headed for Uganda. She was off to teach at a school operated there by the Holy Cross Congregation, the religious order that operates Notre Dame.

The man was off to Uganda to work on a Bible translation project. While waiting in line for the plane's bathroom, he asked the young Catholic student what she was doing. Then, he hit her with the loaded question: "Are you saved?"

"No," responded Nussbaum without missing a beat. "I'm Catholic."

The encounter did not end there, of course. Nussbaum, being the bright young Catholic that she is, had a ready retort, at least in her own imagination. But as happens in many encounters, the best retort is not ready at the moment. It took her some time to remember Matthew 25, a vivid description of the Final Judgment in which Jesus proclaims that you won't get into heaven by proclaiming how you were born again, but by whether you visited the imprisoned, fed the hungry, and helped the least of your fellow humans.

"What you did not do for one of these least ones, you did not do for me," says Jesus, one of the handful of scriptural quotations in which he describes the details of salvation.

Nussbaum writes: "I still wonder. Why don't I

get saved? Why don't I welcome the stranger, or visit the imprisoned, or console the doubtful, or forgive offenses willingly?"

We will encounter Ms. Nussbaum later. But first, the broader question.

Despite these increased cultural contacts—and maybe because of them—never before in our country's history has the evangelical/non-evangelical gap loomed so large. Frequently, often through cultural conflicts, non-evangelicals are mixing it up with the evangelical world, only to find themselves perplexed and sometimes angry at what is perceived as a lack of tolerance and a worldview that seems foreign. This has always been true in the Bible Belt; now it's become even more apparent in blue state areas.

Two examples:

Tim LaHaye and Jerry B. Jenkins's *Left Behind* series of best-selling books and videos portray a world where Jesus has returned and the salvation of the elect is taking place. "The elect" clearly excludes Jews, Catholics and others. In fact, the unsaved perish in particularly squeamish ways. (One teenage girl I know, raised in an evangelical household, has largely been shielded from television sex and violence but gets a particular pleasure out of the more violent parts of the *Left Behind* series.) Only after the books had sold more than 40 million copies (the equivalent of several Harry Potter books) did mainstream media begin to take notice. Only 8 percent of its sales have occurred in the Northeast, where I live, and where most of my acquaintances have never heard of the books. In the South, LaHaye and Jenkins are celebrities. If you mentioned their names at a Catholic gathering, however, few people would recognize them.

 When President George W. Bush responded to a question from author Bob Woodward testifying that he sought advice from his Heavenly Father, as well as his earthly father, the former president, voters in many parts of the country were left scratching their heads. What kind of political leader talks so freely about communicating with the Almighty, they wondered. Who can have such a chummy relationship with the Deity?

It is a language that one doesn't hear on the West Side of Manhattan, or even in the neighborhoods of Queens where I live.

Media interest in the evangelical world reached its zenith during the 2004 presidential campaign. There had been spurts of interest before, particularly during the 1976 election campaign during which evangelical Jimmy Carter emerged on the national scene. Yet Carter, as a moderately liberal Democrat, was able to reach out in those areas where evangelicals were not very strong. In Bush's case, the division between the Catholic/Jewish parts of the country—the so-called blue states clustered on the coasts and around the industrial Great Lakes vs. the red states in the West and South with a strong evangelical flavor—was never so stark.

What kind of political leader talks so freely about communicating with the Almighty? Blue Staters wondered.

A PBS *Frontline* report aired in April of that year focused on Bush's evangelical roots. As Bush was shown talking to evangelical audiences sharing how "Jesus changed my heart" from his days as a young man with an alcohol problem to his born-again conversion during a weekend talk with Dr. Billy Graham, I could identify the language as one I'd heard from evangelicals in many settings. As a religion writer, I'd heard the lingo many times at crusades and in churches, as well as in discussions with evangelicals. To me, it was like a foreign language. I'd gotten to the point where I could understand it, even if I was not fluent enough to speak it. The president, a man with roots in the Ivy League Northeast, has obviously mastered the dialect from his Texas experience.

So it was not too unusual to me. But I watched the program with a friend, a true blue stater and fervent non-Bush voter, who provided a running commentary on that language. "Oh God, how sickening!" she said. "That sounds like bullsh** to me," she proclaimed as Bush opened his soul to his evangelical confreres. She adamantly agreed with Jim Wallis, an evangelical with a strong social justice bent, who was quoted on the program as saying that Bush's embrace of evangelical theology, combined with his aggressive military posturing around the world, offered "a framework of the misuse of religion."

Liberal columnist Nicholas Kristof of the *New York Times* noted in an April 2004 piece that evangelicals are one of the few groups left who are considered socially acceptable in liberal circles to attack. He notes the prevalence of such items as T-shirts emblazoned with the slogan: "So Many Right-Wing Christians . . . So Few Lions." While blue-state intellectuals are not completely devoid of religion—many dabble in Buddhism, for example—few have a working knowledge of evangelicals, notes Kristof, who wrote that evangelicals are involved in a much wider range of activities than their stereotypical ones, such as opposing gay rights. They have, for example, been among the most vocal in highlighting human rights horrors taking place in Africa, such as in Sudan, usually far away from the mainstream media radar screen.

Evangelicals are all over, and they defy the stereotypes. According to the Barna Research Group, which does hefty research on evangelical life, about 20 percent of Americans are evangelical. Three-quarters are white and married; a third are baby boomers; more than half live in the South, and 36 percent volunteer to help with their church, compared to 24 percent of other Americans. They exceed the national average in college graduation rates, taking to task the image of evangelicals as a bunch of ignorant yahoos. Because they are more likely to have large families, marketers see them as a largely untapped market that is just beginning to be discovered.

If we were to take seriously the uptake in coverage of evangelicals after the 2004 election, we'd think evangelicals were everywhere spiking in numbers and influence. Both militant secularists and evangelicals sometimes have an incentive to keep this myth alive. But it is largely mythology. We may not be as hyper-religious a country as some make us out to be.

Dave Olson of *TheAmericanChurch.org* has sought to clarify the numbers. He uses figures from a variety of sources, including the Glenmary Fathers, a Catholic community devoted to ministry in the Bible Belt who have studied where the so-called "unchurched" are. While some surveys say that 40 percent of Americans attend church every weekend, Olson takes another approach. Through studies of various denominations, he's found there's a huge gap between what people tell pollsters they do on Sunday and what they actually do.

Olson, an evangelical Christian, wants to make the point that there's a whole lot of untended sheep on the American landscape ready to hear the gospel. On any given weekend, only about 19 percent of us are in church. And only about a quarter of Americans "attend church regularly"—by that he means at least three out of the last eight Sundays, a rather liberal standard.

Of those most active, however, it is the evangelicals who make the largest impact. Out of every 10 churches formed each year, nine are evangelical. Still, this church building is largely a response to the movement of population. He estimates that only 9 percent of the population attends evangelical churches, a slight drop from 1990. Catholics are said to be roughly 25 percent of the population, but only 6 percent of the population are attending Mass on any weekend. That number has also declined.

So, instead of coming over the hills ready to take over the culture, devoted, practicing Christians are a small slice of the wider population. But they're a significant slice, and a counter-cultural one. Catholics share in some of that counter-cultural stance. It's clear that evangelicals and Catholics, at least those segments who consider themselves the most fervent, and what outsiders see as the most conservative, are coming together over political concerns.

I once worked for an upstate New York Catholic newspaper during the height of the Opera-tion Rescue efforts, in which opponents of abortion would blockade entrances to abortion facilities and risk arrest. It was an attempt to galvanize the pro-life movement just as the Civil Rights movement had been galvanized some 20 years before.

When I went to my first such action, in the small upstate city of Hudson, I expected to see lots of Roman collars. Instead, the protest was led by young men in plaid shirts with bullhorns, many with Italian last names. They were former Catholics, now evangelical ministers, exhorting crowds to a cause that resonated with their Catholic background. The evangelical/Catholic alliance, particularly among conservative political activists, was beginning to coalesce. On that frigid morning in upstate New York, it was obvious that we were a long way from "Rum, Romanism and Rebellion."

Father Richard Neuhaus, editor of the journal *First Things* and prolific writer, is a former Lutheran pastor and now a priest of the New York Catholic Archdiocese. A former anti-Vietnam War activist, he has spent most of his latter career taking the opposite side of issues from his friends from the radical '60s.

Over the past ten years, he has developed a close friendship with Chuck Colson, the former Nixon aide, prison reformer, and fervent lay evangelical preacher. They came together to produce the document titled *Evangelicals and Catholics Together*, outlining where evangelicals and Catholics unite and divide.

Father Neuhaus conceded to the *New York Times* that culturally and religiously, he frequently finds himself on the "other" side of the evangelical/others divide. "There is much in the evangelical culture that grates against me—the overly confident claims to being born again, the forced happiness and joy, the awful music." It was the kind of statement that, if uttered by anyone else, would generate some flak from the evangelical world. But rare for a Catholic priest, Father Neuhaus is cut some slack in those circles.

He's willing to endure what he considers the bad music (actually, to many outsiders comfortable with American pop music styles of country and gospel, the music is one of the more endearing parts of the evangelical service) for its political benefits. He said the alliance growing between evangelicals and conservative Catholics—particularly on issues such as abortion and opposition to gay marriage—is a positive dynamic in U.S. politics and cultural life.

It's not only those issues that would be considered "conservative" that are uniting Catholics and evangelicals. A coalition of Catholic and evangelical groups was able to persuade the Bush administration to increase funding for AIDS programs in Africa. And it's been the evangelicals who have pushed the plight of black Sudanese Christians into the media spotlight. As evangelicals become more involved in foreign missions, they are bringing back to America some of the grassroots concerns of the poor. It's a bit like how Catholic missionary groups, such as Maryknoll, galvanized opposition to U.S. policy in Central America in the 1980s. They returned from foreign lands with tales to tell, and found American audiences to be largely sympathetic.

That alliance on the big issues is also being felt in other ways. Catholic churches are developing a more evangelical style in response to wide cultural shifts.

St. Stephen's, a Catholic church in Cleveland, is marketing itself in a way reminiscent of aggressive evangelical efforts. Once an aging, dying urban parish, it has taken to building market share, much like evangelical megachurches such as Willow Creek in suburban Chicago.

Much to the diocese's chagrin, parishioners from St. Stephen's put up billboards, pitching their church as "Reverent, Conservative, Uncompromising." Other billboards proclaimed, "Tired of Catholic Compromise?" The diocese objected that the ads implied that other churches were somehow failing to live up to their Catholic beliefs. After all, if St. Stephen's is uncompromising, does that mean that the typical parish in the Cleveland Diocese is compromised?

A group of parishioners who paid for the campaign, however, noted that the only way for St. Stephen's to survive is to market itself to suburban Catholics discontented with local liturgies. They are blatantly appealing to "parish shoppers" seeking the best deal. Catholic parishes, traditionally formed around geographic neighborhoods, are learning to adapt and market themselves, much like their evangelical neighbors have always done. If Catholics have left their neighborhoods, some urban churches are willing to seek them out for Sunday visits, some with a decidedly conservative pitch to nostalgic Catholic roots.

The *Los Angeles Times* reports that some churches in that city are developing a more evangelical style in ministering to Latino immigrants, many of whom have grown accustomed to more emotive prayer styles common in evangelical churches.

At St. Thomas the Apostle Church near downtown Los Angeles, for example, services feature salsa music and the waving of arms in praise of Jesus. At one service a lay preacher, Noel Diaz, prompts an altar call, a mainstay of evangelical culture in which participants come forward to publicly commit themselves to Christ.

At one L.A. church, services feature salsa music and the waving of arms in praise of Jesus.

"My message is that you don't have to go outside the church to have this kind of personal relationship with Jesus," says Diaz, who preaches around the country in similar services geared to keeping Latinos in the Catholic fold.

There is another theological dimension to Catholics becoming more evangelical. The roots of the evangelical style in many Catholic communities grew out of Vatican II's opening for Scripture studies. Everywhere, Catholics have opened up their Bibles, often in small parish groups. While the doctrinal differences remain, Catholics and evangelicals are both becoming familiar with a certain style that includes Scripture study and discussions.

One cannot also underestimate the influence of the Catholic charismatic movement. Begun in the United States in the late 1960s in Catholic colleges such as Duquesne in Pittsburgh, the charismatic movement—with formal Church support—brought Catholics into a style of prayer that borrowed heavily from the Protestant Pentecostal movement. Devout Catholics in prayer meetings would even speak in tongues. I remember as a youth on Long Island how such services fascinated me and attracted thousands of young people, experimenting in the realm of religion much like the wider experimentations going on in the culture of the post-1960s era. That charismatic movement has largely waned in the Catholic Church, but its emphasis on emotionality in prayer and spiritual life lingers.

Influence flows in the other direction as well. Quietly, especially among the growing scholarly community now developing among evangelicals, there is a movement towards incorporating what has always been seen as Catholic beliefs into evangelical practice. In many evangelical churches, the time of the year has little impact on the service, except for obvious exceptions such as Christmas and Easter. The preacher decides what Scriptures are relevant, with little reference to the liturgical cycle valued for centuries by Catholics, Orthodox Christians, and liturgically minded Protestants. This is one of the features of the evangelical service most jarring to Catholics, who are rooted in the liturgical seasons, often in an unconscious way. I never realized how important that aspect of faith was to me until I went to churches that did not observe the different liturgical seasons. As someone who has been imbued in a liturgical vision, I find joyous singing in the middle of Lent, for example, highly disconcerting.

That is changing. Now some evangelical churches are observing Lent by the marking of foreheads on Ash Wednesday. Some are lighting candles during Advent. Bob Wenz, U.S. ministries director with the National Association of Evangelicals, quoted by the Associated Press, notes that evangelicals are now "focusing more on the sensory aspects of worship rather than on the cognitive aspects." As we saw at Holy Land in Orlando, evangelicals embrace Passion plays. At multiplexes across the country, they flocked to Mel Gibson's *The Passion of the Christ* and its Catholic iconography of the Blessed Mother, based upon the reflections of a contemplative German nun. Under the radar, a sacramental imagination is quietly, slowly developing among evangelicals. At the same time, Catholics regularly gather in Scripture study groups around the country, much like those that have long existed in evangelical churches.

Catholic language is beginning to seep into the evangelical world. For example, when President Bush and others invoke the "culture of life" phrase when they oppose abortion, they are citing language developed by Pope John Paul II.

Perhaps the most startling evidence of evangelicals' interest in things Catholic was seen on the cover of *Time* on March 21, 2005. It described the intense interest among Protestants in general, and evangelicals in particular, about that consummate icon of Catholicism, Mary, the mother of Jesus.

Over the past few decades, more evangelicals are discovering, Mary plays such a vital role in the Gospels that she can't be ignored, playing more prominent a role there than any character except Jesus himself. No longer is she seen as the idolatrous figment of Catholic religious imagination. The influence of Hispanics on American culture is also beginning to be felt as the Virgin of Guadalupe and other visions of Marian devotion become an integral part of wider Christian, not only Catholic, culture. There are nearly eight million Hispanics in America who consider themselves Protestant, and that number is growing. They have brought into those churches, many of them evangelical, their Catholic conscious- ness honoring Mary. And, of course, Gibson's film featured Mary as a prime player, riveting evangelical audiences around the country.

Another quiet influence on evangelicals' views on Mary and other things Catholic is intermarriage. One Marian Protestant devotee, interviewed by *Time*, has been married to a Catholic for 17 years. He's caught on to Marian devotion. He thinks that the common evangelical bracelet that asks, "What Would Jesus Do?" should have a companion piece asking, "How Would Mary React?" Evangelicals are increas- ingly finding that Mary, in her faithful acceptance of God's will for her, remains a faith model for all Chris- tians, not just Catholics.

Evangelicals are also looking at Catholic Church leadership, even during an era of ghastly priest sex abuse scandals, in a more positive light. Mark Noll, an historian at evangelical Wheaton College, noted in a *Boston Globe* column that the pontificate of Pope John Paul II transformed relations between Catholics and evangelicals in the U.S.

When John Kerry, a Catholic, ran for president, it was conservative evangelicals who were most vocally hoping that he would obey the Vatican line on abortion and other culturally conservative issues. This was a far cry from the campaign of John Kennedy, who faced charges from evangelicals that he would be dominated by Rome!

Noll cites "an ecumenism of the trenches" that has linked evangelicals and many conservative Catholics, particularly in opposition to abortion and gay marriage. But, he says, the link is more than simply political. It has moved into culture as well.

Evangelicals buy albums by Catholic troubadour and lay monk John Michael Talbot. At World Youth Day events, an extravaganza sponsored by the Catholic Church which brings together hundreds of thousands of young people, the famous "Jesus Film," a production by the evangelical Campus Crusade for Christ, is regularly shown. While there has been much publicity about the political alliances, these cultural shifts are, in the long-run, more important, says Noll. When Catholics and evangelicals talk regularly about the Bible, prayer, and the person of Jesus, they are overcoming the antagonisms that grew out of the Reformation and foreseeing a new age of Christian unity. This is ecumenism at the grassroots, often not sanctioned or acknowledged by official discussions between churches—a difficult task because of the loose authority structure of the evangelical movement.

It's not as if this evangelical tilting towards Catholicism makes everyone happy, of course. We're not all ready to join hands and sing KumBaYah. Signs of friction abound. A website based in Michigan operated by Way of Life, an evangelical ministry, notes the popularity of Catholic spirituality authors such as Thomas Merton and inveighs against it.

"The Lord Jesus warned about repetitious prayers, and He gave no liturgy to the churches apart from the simple ordinances of baptism and the Lord's Supper. There is no New Testament pattern for the use of rote prayers, chanting, ringing bells, wearing special clothes, lighting candles, and such things," warned the website author, chagrined about this trend.

Fuzzy, warm ecumenism is also absent from other evangelical sources as well. A recent report from the Southern Baptist International Mission Board supported that denomination's outreach in Catholic countries. "Why would we invest such efforts in Catholic countries?" asked a church official, noting that nearly 1,200 Southern Baptist missionaries are active in 65 predominantly Catholic countries. "It is," he adds bluntly, "because they are lost."

It remains a difficult task to chart how attitudes change. Evangelicals may have become so numerous that, much like Catholics, they have melted into the rest of the culture. While much coverage focuses on how different evangelicals are from the rest of us, a growing body of research indicates that evangelicals increasingly are part of mainstream America. While this horrifies liberals, it also scares evangelical leaders, who worry that their community may become seduced by the blandishments of our media culture. They prefer a community that stands apart, a remnant allied against the corrosive forces of secularism.

A recent survey by *U.S. News and World Report* noted that evangelicals admired the late Pope John Paul II—59 percent gave the pontiff high ratings— while only 44 percent had a favorable view of the Rev. Jerry Falwell, the Christian Right firebrand. Those speakers at the Republican National Convention in 1884 who invoked "Romanism" as a plague must be spinning in their graves!

And it appears that evangelicals have adopted

the live-and-let-live attitudes prevalent in the wider American culture. Only about 50 percent of evangelicals surveyed believe that only their fellow evangelicals will go to heaven. This fact threatens some evangelical leaders, who assert that an exclusive vision of salvation, open only to those who proclaim faith in a personal Christ, is essential to evangelical belief. It parallels the concerns of Pope Benedict XVI and other church leaders that Catholics, particularly in wealthy countries, have fallen into an easygoing relativism on moral and doctrinal issues.

Ronald J. Sider, president of Evangelicals for Social Action and a seminary professor, worries that evangelicals are in danger of melting into the rest of American culture. Writing in *Christianity Today*, Sider sees some alarming signals about evangelical life. He echoes much of what one reads about how Catholics have picked up some bad habits from the wider culture.

For example: evangelicals are as likely to get divorced as anyone else, problematic to those who say that Jesus' teachings against divorce (Matthew 19:4–6) ought to be followed. While evangelical opposition to gay marriage has earned widespread headlines, it's apparent that heterosexual evangelicals, and Catholics for that matter, are having as much difficulty with marriage as anyone.

Evangelicals are urged to tithe. In reality, notes Sider, they contribute just more than four percent to their churches. He notes that when it comes to pornography, evangelical men are absorbed in it as deeply as others. To his credit, Sider expands his warning signals beyond the usual suspects of sex and money. White evangelicals, he is much chagrined to learn about, are more likely to object to living next door to an African American family than other religious groupings are.

Sider emphasizes that evangelicals need to create alliances with the poor and the disenfranchised in American culture. He is proof that not all evangelicals are politically conservative. *Sojourners*, under the guidance of Jim Wallis, is both a magazine and social service community based in Washington that has long provided a voice for evangelicals who believe the first order of politics should be a compassionate stance towards the poor. Like much of the Catholic press, the magazine is as likely to chide pro-choice politicians, as well as those who would cut aid to the poor in return for lower tax rates on the rich.

David Brooks, the mildly conservative columnist

for the *New York Times*, has spent a career as a trend spotter. Although Jewish himself, he has chronicled various religious alliances he sees emerging in the Christian world. One in particular intrigues him: the growing cooperation between liberals concerned with world poverty and evangelical pastors who are rushing to their cause.

The presence of the rock superstar and world development guru Bono at various evangelical churches is a sign of this, notes Brooks. Bono has discovered the energy and interest in such places as Rick Warren's Saddleback Church in southern California. Warren, the author of the mega-bestseller *The Purpose Driven Life*, has urged his congregants to get involved in causes such as African debt relief and AIDS. While routinely castigated in many media circles for its adherence to right-wing politics, the social gospel may well be ready to take off among evangelicals who, as always, bring enthusiasm and treasure to their causes.

Jeffrey Johnson, a Texas native and evangelical interviewed for *The American Prospect* and a classics graduate student at Princeton, notes that an intense interest in the Scriptures often results in a commitment to the cause of social justice. Those who know and understand the Gospels, he says, cannot ignore their regular references to the importance of helping the poor and the oppressed.

"It sounds paradoxical, but holding (the Scriptures as the inspired word of God)—often considered a more theologically conservative position—can land one to pretty progressive political territory. What do we do with verses that talk about God's concern for the poor, the oppressed, orphans, widows and the immigrants in our midst. Do we just ignore these?"

What do we do with verses about God's concern for the poor and the oppressed?

Despite these progressive strains, various surveys do indicate that evangelicals are more conservative than the rest of us (and the pollsters reminded us, *ad nauseum*, how white evangelicals provided the push for President Bush's 2004 electoral victory). Evangelicals remain more likely, for example, to oppose gay marriage and abortion than even Catholics, who have a centralized Church authority opposed to such measures. That clinging to traditional values earned evangelicals increasing media attention and, in some circles, increased fear and loathing. It seemed that for better and worse, evangelical reach was moving into quarters of American life it had never penetrated before.

These new developments caused me to reflect upon how that influence had made an impact on my own spiritual pilgrimage.

Finding Jesus Far
from the Bible Belt

Besides the news coverage of the 2004 election focused on the evangelical/non-evangelical split in the
American public, my interest in the question evolved
as a number of events converged in my life. I had
spent nearly 20 years in the diocesan Catholic press.
It was work I enjoyed in many ways. I can't think of

any better way to make a living than telling the stories of people responding to faith.

Yet, as one wag described it to me, those who love Chinese food are better off not knowing what goes on in the kitchen. It got to be the same with my relationship with the Catholic Church. I loved its teachings, felt truly inspired by what it had to say, and even tried to live up to its ideals as much as possible. Almost all of what I knew about religious faith was incorporated into the Catholic experience. I was a cradle Catholic and proud of it. But, even back in 1998, the gathering storms of scandal were about to envelop the Church. There were too many rumblings about how people were mistreated, about massive hypocrisy. I heard too many stories I could never write or describe in the diocesan press, or for that matter even in the secular press.

There was an earthquake engulfing the Church that would shake its very being. I wanted to opt out of regular Catholic Church employment, in large measure to save my own faith.

So I landed a job as an editor with the *American Bible Society* magazine (once you get into the religion biz, it ain't easy getting out of it). As a result, I became immersed in evangelical culture, a strange and alien world with its own codes, language and mores.

The American Bible Society (ABS) has spent most of its nearly 190-year history with a mission devoted to spreading the Word of God in the most appealing way possible. Its scriptural translations have emphasized simplicity and modern usage, with a focus on presenting the Bible to people who had never really studied it before. It was a mission I could be comfortable with.

What also interested me about the ABS was its culture. Although located just a few blocks from New York City's Central Park and Lincoln Center, it reeked of American old-time evangelical religion. While Bible Society leaders frequently quoted business jargon and our offices exerted a corporate feel and identity, employment there was very different from other kinds of office places.

For one thing, employees would regularly gather as a staff to hear preaching and singing in a style very different from what most jaded New Yorkers experienced. Catholics had been on its board since the 1970s, and many of its middle-management people, like myself, were Catholics and members of mainstream Protestant denominations. But the culture and leadership were decidedly evangelical in approach and theology. This was evident even in small things, such as the "no alcohol" policy for the office site, including business lunches and meetings. By contrast, in Catholic culture alcohol consumption is largely taken for granted—perhaps too much so.

There were other reminders of the difference in cultural worlds. A simple statement placed in the magazine I edited declared that Bible stories may not be literally historically true. This statement was mild by Catholic biblical scholarship standards, but the ruckus it caused among Bible Society supporters caught me completely off-guard. I had allowed a cultural norm to be violated. We were besieged by thousands of letters. I was told in no uncertain terms that a non-literal approach to the Scriptures would not be tolerated in the magazine; as far as the American Bible Society was concerned, the evangelical conservative way was really the only way to look at the Scriptures.

Frequently I'd have discussions with co-workers about their beliefs. And all in all, I enjoyed those discussions. I was learning a new culture, becoming imbued in its language. It was a language I wasn't particularly comfortable speaking—I could never make the requisite references to "heart" feelings frequently required by that lingo—but I was beginning to understand it. I had to give them credit—here were people who knew the Scriptures and were willing to apply its lessons to their lives. They seemed sure of where they were going and their place in the world.

And then 9/11 happened. What can cause a greater faith crisis than when two airliners explode into a skyscraper complex? There was a lot of brave talk in New York in those days, but much of that seemed to mask profound angst and uncertainty that the jingoistic chatter from politicians could not assuage.

The evangelical certitude at the American Bible Society began to wear on me. Being in the midst of New York City in those times caused some to cling to certitudes. I had the opposite reaction. I became less certain about everything.

There are so many stories from that day, and mine is not unusual. As I watched from my office cubicle on a television monitor the horrors taking place at the World Trade Center just six miles away, I was fielding calls from my wife's relatives. She had a cousin, Yvonne, who worked in the Towers. My wife has no sister, and Yvonne has been a kind of kid sister. Yvonne's mother, my wife's aunt, kept calling me from Florida asking me if I knew anything. And, of course, I knew as little as anyone else. As I looked at the television screen, I couldn't believe that anyone would survive. I called Yvonne's apartment, and there was only a tape machine. She had left for work. We found out that afternoon that Yvonne was one of those who had escaped more than 70 floors that day. It was another small miracle that seemed to abound that day amid the tragedies.

As I walked across the Queensborough Bridge that afternoon with tens of thousands of other New Yorkers stranded by the catastrophe, I watched from afar as the Towers threw out their debris and smoke. It was no longer just a flickering image on a television set. I couldn't help reflecting that if it had happened just two weeks before. . . . My then 21-year-old daughter, Audrey, had just weeks before leaving for a semester in Spain interned with Morgan Stanley, a downtown stock firm located right next door to the Towers. My 19-year-old son Pierce had spent a number of days that summer at the Twin Towers doing business with an employment agency headquartered there. He, luckily, was also away at college by September 11.

For weeks afterwards the streets of New York were filled with photocopied posters of men and women accompanied by the plaintive question, "Have you seen . . .?" To those posters gradually were added flowers and candles, like the mini-shrines that we've become accustomed to around accident sites. It all seemed so Catholic, this inclination to construct shrines to the dead. All around the city the streets were filled with shrines, many of them dedicated to heroic firefighters but many more simply physical reminders of the many young people who'd just begun their careers in the world of New York finance.

It all seemed so Catholic, this inclination to construct shrines to the dead.

While the media was filled with tales of heroism the next few weeks, I couldn't get over the apparent arbitrariness of the entire event. In response, we had regular prayer sessions at the ABS. We were told unceasingly that God was watching over us. But I wasn't buying it. Gradually, the facile expressions of faith in a loving God began to make little sense to me. I fled across the street to St. Paul's Church, a Catholic parish run by the Paulist Fathers, for the comfortable ritual of the noon liturgy, where attempts to explain the unfathomable were largely left to God. At that Mass I never felt more Catholic and more consoled by the traditions that I ordinarily take for granted. Catholics, I thought, have a knack for mourning and a sense of mystery that gives believers a glimpse into coping with heartbreak.

Still, I couldn't get over the basic certitude and goodness of the people I knew at the ABS. They had a sense of being saved. They had a sense that in some strange mysterious way, even in this atrocity God was present. It was a faith I had to admit I did not share, at least not in the same way. Those thoughts lingered after I left the ABS in the spring of 2003, the result of a massive layoff.

I spent that summer of 2003 at Northwestern University near Chicago, part of a group of 10 religion journalists. With the help of a grant from the Lilly Foundation, we studied all the major religious groups, from Buddhists to Scientologists, that make up the pluralistic American religion scene. The Chicago area was our laboratory, and we learned about everything from what Sikhs believe, to Scientologists' methods for healing painful memories, to how Mormons revere their dead ancestors.

It was a mind-bending and soul-stretching experience. We would hear lectures and discussions about each religious group's beliefs and history, then we would spend the afternoon visiting the group. I came in thinking I knew a lot. I concluded that I knew little, and found myself attracted to expressions of religious faith that had little to do with my reflex Catholicism.

After every study session and visit we would talk about our experiences. In all of that religious mix, living the American religious smorgasbord in a way few will ever experience, what struck me most were the negative feelings among most of my fellow students directed at evangelical Christians. This was at the height of the sex abuse scandal revelations, and I assumed Catholics would be the main target of anger and distrust. What really turned off the visiting scholars, however, was the certitude expressed by the evangelical Christians we visited.

After all, we were immersed in the questioning tradition of journalism. Most participants were just starting out, trying to get a foothold on the bottom rungs of the media industry. About half of us came from Catholic backgrounds, although formal religious observance was spotty. Besides a few from Jewish backgrounds, the rest of us, particularly those who were raised in and near the evangelical tradition, shuddered after we would visit those groups. Catholics, it turns out, had no monopoly on angst and long-hidden memories.

The strongest reaction occurred after our visit to various evangelical churches and institutions. One was the city's Moody Church, where we were greeted by its pastor, Dr. Erwin W. Lutzer, the author of scores of books on all sorts of theological questions. He spent an afternoon with us, fielding inquiries about everything from "can gay people marry?" to "can non-Christians be saved?" (The answer to both was a resounding No.) He did not lack for confidence or apparent biblical evidence for the sureness of his views.

Moody is a strong and old evangelical community. Its sanctuary in downtown Chicago is filled by thousands every Sunday. The building is spare, somewhat like an old gymnasium, complete with arena-style seating, perfect for the austere preacher proclaiming the Word so well-known in traditional evangelical circles.

I'd heard Dr. Lutzer's series of certitudes proclaimed by other conservative preachers, and thought little of it. It was what I expected from Dr. Lutzer, whose old-fashioned glasses and austere manner fit the image of the stern preacher he appeared to be. But his certitude left our group shaking and arguing for hours afterwards. Those of us who know good people who are not professing Christians were unwilling to concede that they are condemned. Those of us trained as questioning journalists wondered how anyone could be so sure about hot-button social issues such as gay marriage. He violated the journalistic credo that all questions and controversies are by definition open-ended.

After his visit to Moody, Ron Csillag, a former Northwestern journalism fellow and Toronto correspondent for Religion News Service, muttered under his breath, "all this fuss over a Jewish carpenter!" Lutzer responded to his inquiries with two of his books. The reverend had a book he had written for every possible question. "I simply recall a man very rigid in his beliefs, who hewed to that old time religion, and the belief that anyone who has not been saved ain't getting into heaven. That includes anyone not like him, most of the planet," recalls Ron. This evangelical claim to exclusivity, and its unabashed expression, is what is downright spooky to many of us on the outside.

Others in the class were offended by our field trip to the famous Willow Creek megachurch deep in the Chicago suburbs. There, more than 5,000 seats are filled each Sunday and Wednesday nights. People come to hear a down-home sermon—the one we heard featured many vignettes about the travails of adolescent sports programs—and lively music with the words flashed on screens. The Wednesday night service we attended featured a pre-program dinner at a giant food court that looked like any other mall food court dotting the American suburban landscape. The church offered little in overt religious symbolism. There were no icons. No stained-glass windows. Here was a group that wanted to fit into the anonymous mid-American suburban landscape—quite deliberately so, as its literature told us.

We were told that the church relies on small groups that offer support and spiritual sustenance. It was an obvious effort to minister in American suburbia where mobility guaranteed that many families lacked a sense of wider community. Isolated in their development cul-de-sacs, with entertainment needs filled by cable television and video games, the American suburbs are filled with families regularly relocated by corporate masters who move middle-level execs around the country. Willow Creek provided a means to reach these mobile families and bring them into a caring community. I felt upbeat after my visit— not so impressed by the theology, which was relatively mundane fare about family life, but encouraged that someone was taking the spiritual needs of American suburbia seriously. My fellow journalism students, however, felt the entire setup reeked of manipulation. Particularly in this cleverly packaged manifestation, which was far slicker than Rev. Lutzer's old-time religion. That anti-evangelical feeling was a theme that permeated our entire summer.

Fewer churches these days embrace the old-time religion of the Moody Church. The Willow Creek model has become the one used by evangelical pastors around the country, particularly in high-growth "exurbs," regions far away from central cities that are booming as Americans continue to spread out in the search for cheaper housing and space.

One such community, described by Jonathan Mahler*, is the Radiant Church in Surprise, Arizona. Led by Pastor Lee McFarland, Radiant Church is a masterstroke of religious marketing.

---

*In the March 27, 2005 issue of the *New York Times* Magazine

As in Willow Creek, the churchy aspects of religion are downplayed. Rock music is the norm, casual attire is Sunday wear, and congregants are provided with self-help sessions to deal with family and other crises. It is marketed as the church-as-mall, and in a new community where there are few shared institutions, it's a hit. On Easter Sunday, Radiant attracts as many as 15,000 worshipers. Megachurch evangelicals

Radiant Church is marketed as the church-as-mall.

have obviously learned to connect with American consumer culture and meet needs that other more traditional churches rarely think about. They are light on overt political involvement, sometimes light on Scripture references, and heavy on ways to deal with practical issues, such as money matters and how to get along with your spouse and children. To me, they fill a spiritual void. To many of my classmates at Northwestern, some of whom were long scarred by bad experiences with evangelicals, the megachurch concept seems like Madison Avenue marketing, not spiritual outreach.

Upon returning home to New York later that summer, I looked with new eyes at how much that evangelical style had permeated regions unheard of years ago. It was obvious that self-help philosophy had permeated Catholic precincts, even those far from the Bible Belt, in ways I hadn't thought about before.

My mother, as staunch a Catholic as anyone I've ever known, was dying from lung cancer. Hers was a Catholicism reared in the Brooklyn parish where she was raised, and nurtured in the Long Island suburbs where my five siblings and I grew up. It was not a showy piety, but we all knew that if you wanted to find the ultimate answers to life's riddles, you found it in the wide embrace of the Roman Catholic Church. Sure, some in my family wandered away from the church, at least for a while, but no one would ever consider joining a different religious group.

Her dying was a long process, taking over a year from that diagnosis until her death on a snowy December night. It mercilessly sapped her strength, took her weight away, and eventually made every breath an achievement. But the time was also merciful. She spent it consciously preparing to die. And she did so in a way that, while true to her Catholic beliefs, was in many ways borrowed, from the models of community provided by the Willow Creek Church and other evangelical congregations in tune with modern American life.

The traditional model of how Catholics die usually included a visit from a priest right before the death, sometimes accompanied by the anointing of the sick during the process. And my mother was getting that.

But she was also dying in a way familiar to me in my days at the American Bible Society and in the glimpses I saw at Willow Creek. She was being prayed over, and she was studying the Scriptures with people from her parish, St. Anne's in Garden City, New York. Sometimes just a few people, sometimes more than a dozen, the group reflected each week in my parents' home. They would talk about the Scriptures and listen to both popular and church music, one of my mother's passions. Like evangelicals, Catholics are beginning to discover that the church isn't the only place to pray.

A journal my mother kept in her final year is filled with easygoing references to the Scriptures: Simon of Cyrene carrying the cross, Abraham starting out in faith, the stories of Jesus' healing miracles. It's the kind of easygoing familiarity with biblical characters shared by the evangelicals at Willow Creek or at Moody Church.

"I think about how far we have all come, how

we can talk openly about so many things," my mother wrote. "A few months ago, we couldn't. Now topics such as cancer, death, suffering, holding on and letting go, grace, the Spirit, and faith, hope and love all come so easily to us," she wrote in her journal about her small prayer support community. These are words an evangelical would likely write and feel comfortable with. It was all-purpose Christianity stripped to its barest essentials to deal with the ultimate of mysteries, death.

As my mother's life concluded, I felt she had begun to incorporate the best of both worlds: she had the solace of the Catholic ritual, with its timeless gestures and signs indicating how God is in the unspoken, as well as the evangelical style, where the vivid Christian truths are spoken about openly and with consolation to those who take them seriously. I couldn't help but thinking that in her case she had been saved by this insight. Of that I was certain. But I wanted to find out how we the living can best work out that salvation. First I needed some background. I talked with my old professor, Dr. Jonathan Moore, who has made his life's work the study of the nuances among Christian groups. He spent that summer of 2003 teaching us religious scholar journalism neophytes at Northwestern the differences between evangelicals, fundamentalists, Methodists and Presbyterians, and more importantly, why it all mattered.

Holy and unholy wars

"I don't know if I have been saved.
I haven't died yet. But I do believe
as a matter of faith that I, along
with all of humanity—not just
born-again Christians—have been
redeemed. I am relying on the infi-
nite mercy of God to welcome me

into the heavenly kingdom in spite of many sins and faults over the course of my lifetime, and I expect to find most of the human community there at the same banquet table, since Scripture tells us that God wishes the salvation of all, whether they call on the name of Jesus or not. It is, after all, not the one who says, 'Lord, Lord' who will enter the kingdom, but the one who does the will of God whether they realize it to be the will of God or not."

Father Richard McBrien, University of Notre Dame theologian

Jonathan Moore is a round-faced academic with a sense of humor. Religion is very often discussed in dry, somber tones, but Jonathan brings to the discussion a quiet wit and a passion about his subject. He knows more about the nuances among evangelicals than anyone else I know.

He was one of my professors at Northwestern. At our final class meeting, he made sure we all got some kind of religious memorabilia: I won the Jesus front-seat car attachment. Jonathan earned his doctorate from the University of Chicago, with a specialization in American religious history. He studied under Martin Marty, the Lutheran minister who is perhaps the country's foremost U.S. religious history scholar. When I caught up with Jonathan, he was ready to begin a fellowship at the University of Illinois, not far from the small town where he grew up where the local Methodist church had been a focal point in his life. He is now an associate professor of religious studies at Grinnell College in Iowa.

If he were asked on the street if he were saved, Jonathan would, like any academic, want to get the meaning behind the question. He knows the question is multi-layered and complex. But he's not ready to dismiss it, as many academics frequently are.

Jonathan gets the big picture of where evangelicals fit into our culture. Raised a United Methodist, Jonathan remains engrossed in the Methodist Church. In fact, much of our class was devoted to the debates within United Methodism, where the clashes between evangelicals—read, conservative—and mainstream

Protestants—read, liberal—are perhaps the most pointed of any denomination. Those struggles mirror what is happening in the wider culture. Methodism was a good choice as a laboratory subject to examine how religious and social tensions can afflict one particular denomination, relatively small in number yet vital in the religious history of our country. The Methodists were one of the early groups on the frontier to sponsor revivals that awakened dormant Christian consciousness. They were in the forefront of evangelical consciousness in the nineteenth century.

While the United Methodist Church leadership has a long history of devotion to various progressive causes, there is also another strain of Methodism that is far more culturally attuned to conservative evangelicalism. George W. Bush, for one, is a member of the United Methodist Church. The denomination's 2004 national meeting featured long debates over gay marriage and ordaining gays to the ministry. One conservative group even called for a rupture between the progressives and conservatives, a measure that was voted down. The church had severed before over the issue of slavery in the 1800s. Today's culture wars threaten to create a rupture much like that one. United Methodists, who have their roots in England

69

but have been formed in large part by their American values, cherish democracy in their governing process; as such, they suffer the same pangs of division that the rest of our democracy does. For better or worse, there is no pope to act as a final arbiter on points of doctrine and culture. In Methodism, the man and woman in the pew has a voice that is unheard of in Catholic tradition, and in most other Protestant traditions as well. That causes disputes to be played out in a public, sometimes contentious, manner.

Jonathan notes that evangelicals, growing increasingly influential in the Methodist scene, are a flash point in our culture because they are so certain of their own salvation and how their moral code should be lived out in the wider culture.

"It goes against the grain of our civic tolerance," says Jonathan. During our class, Jonathan would emphasize the shades of differences in belief in the American Protestant tradition. For many Catholics, it is a stew of ambiguity and confusion. Raised in a church that sees its unity in Rome, we are unfamiliar with the history of Protestantism, in which theological arguments resulted in the forming of different sects. Jonathan painstakingly pointed out to us the differences between a Congregationalist and a Unitarian, two older mainstream groups. These denominations fit into a wider culture in which there is a growing tolerance, a society in which religious differences are glossed over or even discounted. But evangelicals work against that grain.

"They are unwilling to relinquish the truth that they think they hold," says Jonathan. Part of that truth involves following the Great Commission given by Jesus at the end of the Gospel of Mark. So they are unable to simply stand aside and let people not know who Jesus is to them.

"It's what they have to do. So they own the truth and spread it as well. They cannot not do it and be good evangelicals," notes Jonathan, who always emphasizes that evangelicals are diverse. There are social justice oriented evangelicals, who tirelessly support liberal-minded programs to assist the poor, an example of which is the Sojourners community based in Washington. There are African American groups, led by dynamic preachers such as T.D. Jakes. There are the "establishment" evangelicals, such as the Rev. Billy Graham, and the religious right of the Christian Coalition and Pat Robertson, politically-minded partisans who garner most of the media hype about evangelicalism.

Evangelicals suffer, much as Catholics do, from stereotyping from outsiders who really don't comprehend the culture. It's something I've seen over many years in the Catholic press. Outsiders, particularly media types, have a tendency to view the Catholic Church as a monolith, in which millions of Catholics receive our instructions from the Vatican and march forth blindly. In this model, Catholicism is a lot like a massive multinational, with the pope as CEO and the parishes as branch offices.

In reality, Catholicism includes those with disparate authority and opinions about almost everything under the sun. There are liberal bishops and conservative bishops. The pope sometimes differs with his own Curia. American Catholic voters are regularly viewed by experts as a crucial swing group in every national election, too diffuse to truly categorize. In fact, some scholars of religion refer to Catholicism as the Hinduism of Christianity, because it is infused with so many different schools of prayer, ritual and perspective, much like the native and diverse religions of India now referred to under the single rubric of Hinduism.

Evangelicals, united on certain doctrinal tenets, have their own diversity. Mark Galli, managing editor

of *Christianity Today*, has put together a chart outlining the evangelical world. It ranges from the
"establishment"—old-timers such as Billy Graham—to Hispanic and African American churches,
as well as the Religious Right of James Dobson and
Pat Robertson, and "seeker
churches" such as Willow
Creek in suburban Chicago.

Catholicism includes those with disparate opinions about almost everything under the sun; evangelicals have their own diversity.

The evangelical move-
ment has a long and complicated history in America.
Well before it was identified
with the Religious Right, it
was in the lead of movements for the abolition of
slavery and the rights of women. (Yes, it's true, although it's hard to imagine evangelicals today in the
forefront of the women's movement.)

Even the definition of *evangelical* poses problems. The *Encyclopedia of Religion and Society* says
that evangelicals are essentially non-denominational
Protestants steeped in the Puritan-Calvinist tradition.
(One thing I've learned about evangelicals is that they
are, however, wary of historical analysis of their
movement, preferring to be called simply "Christians." It does seem at times that many of the popular

thinkers pretend that 20 centuries of Christian life just did not happen between Pentecost and this very minute when the preacher is postulating a truly renewed Christian life bereft of stodgy tradition.)

They focus on bare essentials of faith. They are non-institutional and non-hierarchical (a quality that makes them look aghast at Catholics). They tend to an exclusionary theology, meaning that they believe that only through Christ can people find God and salvation. (When, as noted earlier, polls indicate that a growing number of evangelicals believe that their non-Christian neighbors can achieve salvation, it's no wonder that some traditionalists find this to be appalling.) So, when they proselytize, a zealous evangelical believes they are simply doing you a favor. They tend to rely solely on the authority of Scripture, but how that is defined is often up for grabs and cause for serious arguments. There is no single person to appeal to on arguments about doctrine. Evangelicals can be part of churches that are independent congregations or they can be part of larger denominations, such as the Southern Baptists, Presbyterians, or Methodists.

Evangelical has its root meaning in the Greek word for *gospel*. During the Reformation, Martin

Luther used it to describe the church he formed in protest of Rome. But in American parlance, it has largely referred to Protestants of a certain stripe. Their roots are in various revival movements that affected Protestantism, both in the nineteenth and twentieth centuries. British historian David Bebbington defines evangelicalism as having four beliefs: lives need to change, the gospel should be spread, Jesus died for our sins, and the Bible should be held as a prime source of God's teaching. Depending upon how you define them, evangelicals comprise between 7 and 47 percent of the U.S. population, but most scholars put the number at 25 percent, roughly the same percentage of Americans who claim to be Catholic.

But what really sets them apart is, as their name suggests, the focus on evangelizing. They believe they have a truth, a view of reality that they cannot keep to themselves if they are to be true to their religious ideals. In that sense, proselytizing is for some evangelicals what keeping kosher is to orthodox Jews. The difference is that the orthodox Jew keeping kosher can largely keep his beliefs to himself or contained within a subculture. Whether or not a particular orthodox Jewish community keeps kosher has little wider cultural implications, except perhaps for shellfish harvesters or pork producers. By definition, proselytizing involves those who may want no part of it.

This can at the least be befuddling or annoying to non-evangelicals, particularly non-Christians. Larry David, the *Seinfeld* co-creator, captured the mindset of many secular Jews. In one episode of the HBO series, *Curb Your Enthusiasm*, in which he plays a character very much like the real Larry David, he complains to his gentile wife about her sister, who married a Jewish man on the condition that he would be baptized an evangelical Christian. He is willing to concede the affection evangelicals have for Jesus, but it perplexes him why they seek converts so aggressively.

"I love lobster," says a very non-kosher Larry David. "But that doesn't mean I go around telling the world that everyone needs to love lobster."

Catholics have on occasion also been forced into a defensive posture regarding evangelical witness. A recent program instituted by the U.S. Military Archdiocese addresses some of these concerns. Although it doesn't mention evangelicals, the program is obviously geared to counteracting the strong evangelical witness that exists in some portions of the military. The U.S. Air Force Academy, for example, has been under investigation by a Pentagon committee for allegedly encouraging evangelical witness—including semi-mandatory chapel sessions—that caused consternation among Jewish students, some of whom were even told that they were responsible for the execution of Jesus. Military proselytizing also disturbs Catholics and mainstream Protestants, who feel they are looked down upon as second-tier Christians in a heavy evangelical culture.

Most of the time that proselytizing is not so crude. But evangelical witness can be particularly effective in the military among those who are at a tender age away from home and contemplating risky overseas assignments.

The military Catholic chaplaincy sponsors a program called Catholics Seeking Christ. It is intended to reinforce the identity of young adult military people as Catholic Christians at a pivotal time in their lives. With the assistance of Paulist Media Works, the Paulist Fathers, the Catholic Leadership Group, and New Group Media, Catholics Seeking Christ offers an ongoing small prayer and discussion group process.

Catholic military personnel gather weekly to read Scriptures, pray, view DVDs, and discuss faith questions, such as "Can a Catholic have a personal relationship with Jesus?" and "How do Catholics read the Bible?" Other topics include the role of the saints in Catholic belief and discerning right and wrong in a Catholic framework. Groups are composed of two leaders and six to eight participants.

The Military Archdiocese is borrowing heavily from evangelicals' techniques to help ward off the temptations of evangelicals seeking to bring military Catholics into their camp.

Still, the most controversial proselytizing evangelicals do is directed in this country towards Jews, who often take exception.

Back in 2001 the *New York Times Magazine* wrote a piece about the Knicks. The story would very well have landed in oblivion—after all, it was just another piece about an over-hyped professional basketball team. But one fact stood out: Eric Konigsberg, the author, who is Jewish, took offense that one of the players he befriended, Charlie Ward, had aggressively proselytized him and said things that he construed as anti-Semitic.

During the course of researching the profile, Konigsberg got friendly with some of the Knicks players, including Ward. After all, he was traveling with the team and established relationships with the players and staff. At the time, players would join together after hard-fought games and pray with their teammates and some of their opponents. The display of Christian piety was being noticed around secular New York. Those who were involved in a Christian prayer group on the team, including Ward, Allan Houston, and Kurt Thomas, invited the writer for a little religious discussion.

Ward asked Konigsberg some theological questions. One of them was "Why did the Jews kill Jesus?", one of the old canards of Christian anti-Semitism. Konigsberg's report of this question caused an odd theological firestorm in the midst of a basketball season. The Anti-Defamation League accused the players of religious bigotry. Ward apologized, saying his comments were not meant to offend any group. It was quickly forgotten.

But Jonathan Moore brought up the flap again at our classes in the summer of 2003 at Northwestern. It was too vivid an example to ignore. Jonathan looked at the controversy quite differently. The ballplayer's questions obviously repeated ancient Christian anti-Semitic notions, true. And many Jews throughout history have been persecuted or even killed by zealous anti-Semites who cloaked their hatreds in religious piety. On the other hand, Jonathan notes, Ward, as a fervent evangelical, is truly compelled to share his religious good fortune with those he cares about. Instead of being offended, author Konigsberg should have appreciated that he meant enough to Ward that he was worth being proselytized, no matter how uncomfortable it made him. The ballplayer cared enough about the sportswriter to engage in a religious dialogue even if Konigsberg felt uncomfortable enough to consider the entire exercise an assault upon his Jewish identity.

Jonathan's views are similar to a commentary that ran in the *Christian Century*, the liberal Protestant journal, at the time of the fracas.

"It's hard not to feel a little sorry for Charlie Ward," noted the editorial writer. "Most of us get our theological lessons in private from sympathetic family, friends or teachers. He got his in public from some angry religious leaders and newspaper columnists."

The editorial conceded that the rebukes were warranted, that the blaming of the Jews as a group for the killing of Jesus is wrong-headed and has caused too much suffering throughout history. But, it noted, " Ward was attempting, in a confused way, to

engage in a Christian-Jewish dialogue." Charlie
Ward, a great athlete—he was a top-flight quarter-
back in college as well as an NBA player—may be
not so gifted as a theologian. But his approach is
something an evangelical Christ-
ian is required to do, even if his
style left much to be desired. This
kind of misunderstanding by
non-evangelicals is common.

> **When evangelicals'
> comments make it
> into the public
> realm, they are
> often attacked.**

When evangelicals' com-
ments make it into the public
realm, they are often attacked. There's a problem
with language. Peter Beinhart, writing in the *New Re-
public* in 2004, wrote that President Bush and his administration were always talking about their "heart"
and the hearts of their political friends and foes. He
wondered if they shouldn't be more concerned about
people's ideas.

But that is a matter of misreading evangelical
language. Evangelicals talk about changes of
"heart" all the time. It was something I heard regularly at the American Bible Society, which frequently
talks about changing hearts as well as minds for the
gospel. For Jonathan, that difference in use of

language often engenders suspicion of evangelicals among the rest of us.

Evangelicals also continue to be attacked for what Jonathan refers to as the "H. L. Mencken" factor. The famous early twentieth-century journalist made his name for his sarcasm directed towards devotees of William Jennings Bryan in the famous Scopes creationist case in the 1920s. His rapier wit is often invoked by secular-minded intellectuals. Mencken devoted much ink to depicting evangelicals as uncouth and uneducated, particularly those who opposed a teacher in tiny Dayton, Tennessee, who had the temerity to talk about theories of evolution in high school biology class. The people protesting evolution were, then as now, easy targets for cosmopolitan sophisticates (as I write this, school boards from California to Pennsylvania continue to argue the merits of intelligent design). That prejudice remains today, even if evangelicals are much closer to the American mainstream than they have ever been. Mencken, by the way, was anti-Catholic as well. He projected the image of the smarmy secularist, locating himself above the ignorant religious mainstream.

Non-evangelists tend toward this same prejudice, but the facts are somewhat more complicated. It was Bryan, after all, the buffoon in Mencken's view, who actually represented Progressive notions about American life, including championing of the poor. Mencken, the darling of free thinkers, suffered from a snobbery that caused him to look down on the economically deprived as well as the religiously fervent and relatively simple people from Tennessee who backed Bryan's fundamentalist defense of the Scripture's creation accounts. Again, evangelical history is more complicated than popular notions often allow. The simple paradigm of "liberal" secularists vs. "conservative" evangelicals frequently falls short under any kind of sophisticated analysis. Those who embrace the evangelical camp do so for diverse and complex reasons, sometimes out of personal theological conviction but also because of historical and cultural currents they may be barely aware of. As Jonathan Moore so well taught us, religious reality is complicated, and why people do what they do with their spiritual lives comes from a complex meshing of tradition, culture, and personal choice. It cannot be determined by simple political labels. The overlap can take place even within the same family—something I have discovered for myself.

5

Two-way conversion traffic

"NO QUESTIONS.
JUST ANSWERS."

sign outside Chestnut Street Community Church in
Roselle, New Jersey

It's Sunday morning, actually early afternoon, at the
Chestnut Street Community Church in Roselle, New
Jersey. I walk in and see about 200 worshipers raising

their hands in prayer and song. Above the sanctuary is a giant screen with the words of the hymn that is entrancing the congregation at the moment.

These days evangelicals have largely left the hymnal behind. It's almost a defining quality. They use large screens to indicate the lyrics. Many of the lyrics, presented through upbeat popular melodies, are repeated over and over. It is like a mantra, although I'm not sure the people in this church would be comfortable with the reference to an Eastern religious practice.

At the front of the church reads a sign: NO QUESTIONS. JUST ANSWERS.

As a Catholic, one is struck by the personal tone of the lyrics. This particular one is about Jesus. Not the historical Jesus, the itinerant preacher who walked through Palestine 20 centuries ago, executed by the ruling authorities after he gathered together a small band of devoted followers who collected his sayings and teachings. No, this is the Jesus these people call upon as an intimate friend who helps them through the turmoil of life in New Jersey in 2004.

"My Savior, my closest friend,
I will worship you until the very end"

It is repeated over and over. The words cascade through the tiny church as the people raise their hands. I am here as the guest of my 24-year-old daughter, Audrey, a fact that startles me and on many levels pleases me.

She is a cradle Catholic. And some of that Catholic baggage shows. She doesn't raise her hands or sing out in an emotive style. For her, church is a place to reflect upon God and hear the Scriptures. She is uncomfortable with emotive displays. And she sheepishly comes strategically late—this service goes on for well over two hours, and for her, church should last about an hour, the usual length of the typical parish Sunday Mass.

If you had told me five years ago that my daughter would be part of an evangelical congregation, I would have said she was more likely to fly to the moon. She is still a political liberal, college grad, occasional singer and dancer conversant in youth culture, and was even a star performer in a hip-hop group formed with chums from her high school days. This is not the stereotypical profile of the clean scrubbed evangelical from the heartland. Yet she finds spiritual sustenance here at Chestnut Street Community on Sundays, one of the few days she can find respite from her high-pressure job at a Manhattan law firm. She works as a para-legal for a retinue of lawyers who, like most lawyers, want everything done yesterday. Overtime is bountiful; an opportunity to reflect and enjoy is not.

Audrey regularly attended Catholic Mass until she was 14, only sporadically thereafter. She grumbled about attending, and her indulgent father—me—figured the development of her faith life was not something he wanted to argue about with a strong-willed teenage daughter every Sunday morning. After adamantly refusing the opportunity to attend Catholic high school, she was admitted to and attended New York City's renowned La Guardia High School for the Performing Arts—the "Fame" school—where she majored in voice. She sang jazz and was part of a school gospel choir. Through her college years at State University of New York at Stony Brook and during a year's study in Spain, she rarely attended church of any kind.

She is like many of her generation. Her involvement with Chestnut Street, a place she came to with her boyfriend Roberto when she moved to New Jersey in early 2004, is, in her mind, not a break with Catholicism. It is, rather, a way for her to join a community based upon the Christianity she was imbued with as a child. Denominational labels don't mean that much to her or many in her generation. Audrey was raised in a diverse religious environment. From me, she experienced Catholicism, and was baptized and educated in the church. But when she visited her maternal relatives, she was exposed to all sorts of Christian styles, including Baptist, Methodist, and Episcopalian.

She credits her Catholic background—she attended Catholic elementary school and regularly attended church with her mother, brother, and myself—as something that reinforced her belief in a higher power.

Yet, she adds, "I never felt at home in the Catholic church." Paradoxically, the church she now belongs to is a "Four Square Church." Its statements of beliefs reaffirm standard evangelical formulations about hell (it exists), about evangelizing (it's a duty for all Christians), and salvation (it comes through Christ alone). Audrey, however, like many of her contemporaries, does not believe that there is a hierarchy of religions, with Christianity more valid than others. She doesn't

"I never felt at home in the Catholic church."

know if she believes in the divinity of Jesus. She is what social theorists describe as a modern American religious searcher. She's the kind of seeker that the Four Square congregation is made for and welcomes, even if its doctrinal statements tend towards the absolute side. Even Pope Benedict XVI might be proud of that: there is no cultural relativism promoted here.

Four Square is a group of congregations scattered around the country, attempting to proclaim the gospel message in a modern way. Their theology may be considered conservative, but Four Square is quick to blend into secular culture for the sake of the gospel.

A Four Square church generally eschews churchy symbols; its services are laid-back, emphasizing personal service. At Chestnut Street, a major focus is on the post-service hospitality, where almost all the congregants mingle for food and coffee and talk. Its history is rooted in the radio preaching of Aimee Semple McPherson, the California radio preacher who won converts across America during the 1930s. While it emphasizes what might be considered a conservative Christian theology, its services are dynamic and emotive. "Four Square" applies to four aspects of Jesus' ministry as Savior, baptizer, healer, and Coming King. Its services emphasize the role of Jesus in the here and now.

Chestnut Street has been led by the husband/ wife ministry team of Art and Sharon Snow for the past three years. They are of my generation, in their late 40s, and came to an awareness of Christianity during the early '70s, when the '60s-influenced Jesus movement and charismatic worship were making inroads into traditional Christian denominations, including Catholicism and Sharon's Methodist Church, where she was raised.

Art came to faith after the travails of living in an alcohol-affected family and living in the streets of Canton, Ohio. Other evangelical-style preachers would focus on their earlier sordid confusion, but Art just lets me know that he came to a conversion after various difficulties.

"I used to live like hell. And then one day it changed," he says, cryptically. I am rather pleased with the pastor leaving a bit of mystery. Too often I've heard evangelicals wallow in their pre-conversion stories. I don't have patience for another tale of woe, a torrent of horror saved at a moment's conversion. I've often concluded that such stories make God's presence in our lives a bit too cut-and-dried. If it was that simple, writers who have chronicled the spiritual life would have little to write about. I'd prefer to let the dark night of the soul remain a mystery.

Pastor Snow's ministry focuses on the music—largely unstructured, free-flowing, almost spontaneous in its personal appeals to God. The service is deliberately unchurchy. There are no hard prayer books to be found. Art doesn't care for printed programs. While he has a sermon ready, he will sometimes break from his prepared text if he believes the Spirit—vital in Pentecostal prayer forms—is moving in a certain direction.

In many ways, he is surprisingly liberal, at least to those who straightjacket evangelicals and Pentecostal leaders. He spent much of the past decade leading a congregation in Washington, D.C. He is an expert in multi-ethnic ministries. While in Washington, he is proud to say, he was welcomed at naming ceremonies held by the parents of Nigerian children.

"I became like an African," he says, noting that the goal of churches should be to embrace varied cultures, much like the missionary Paul, while delivering the gospel at the same time. That goes for modern, pop culture America as well.

I ask him if he believes that those who attend

Holy Land USA

other churches are not saved. He takes the question in a different direction. Taking out a calculator and noting that Roselle has a population of 40,000, he divides that number by the number of churches in town. If everyone was an active Christian, he says, every church would have 3,500 members. Chestnut Street has a membership of 270 and he could not imagine handling a congregation in the thousands. If it grew to that size, it would likely lose the human warmth and support that it now generates. He may well be on to something here: in the best-selling book *The Tipping Point*, Malcolm Gladwell argues that 150 is about the right size for any community to maintain focus and human scale. Pastor Snow is intuitively aware of that argument. Chestnut Street, seemingly a small congregation, particularly for someone used to Catholic parishes in the Northeast with its thousands of weekly worshipers, is actually in danger of becoming too large for the kind of spiritual intimacy it promotes.

Instead of focusing on numbers, he's got a credo for his church to live by: "Love God, Serve People, and Have Fun." Not bad as a summary for the Christian life well lived. And he is quick to emphasize that not all the Christians are in his church or in other

92

churches. "Being in a garage doesn't make you a car. Being in a church doesn't make you a Christian." While evangelical, it is an inclusive kind.

To more conservative Catholic commentators, Audrey's presence at Chestnut Community Church, can be explained by the failure of lukewarm liberal Catholics, like me, to share their faith to a different generation definitely seeking rock-solid answers in a changing world. Audrey, they would say, is seeking that old-time religion because she never really picked up a religious viewpoint at home. They would look at the sign outside the door promising answers, not questions. Many post-Vatican II Catholics, they say, are too much in love with the questions. Humans, especially young people starting out, seek answers. This is a neat and tidy explanation. And like most such neat and tidy explanations, it couldn't be more wrong. Audrey fits into a category that Robert C. Fuller, a professor of religious studies at Bradley University in Illinois, describes as a seeker. We have entered a time, he says, when people are less concerned with denominational labels and are willing to explore the religious marketplace. Americans, he emphasizes, have always been religiously diverse. Now they are even more so.

Audrey, in fact, is actually attracted to Chestnut Street Community by what she sees as its liberalizing elements. For one thing, Pastor Art Snow's ministry relies heavily on his wife, Sharon Snow, and she is a strong presence in the congregation, making announcements and warmly greeting newcomers.

Sharon is quick to greet us after the service. In evangelical churches, you cannot sneak in unnoticed. Invariably, newcomers are asked to rise and introduce themselves to the congregation. The anonymity of most Catholic parishes is unheard of here.

I offer thanks to Sharon for welcoming my daughter to her congregation. When Audrey moved out of our family apartment in Queens and bought a small condo in New Jersey, her mother and I were concerned that it would be hard for her to find a social network on the other side of the river. (In New York terms, the New Jersey side is a place rarely visited, with the exception of football games at Giant Stadium and as a stopover to Philadelphia or Washington.)

I have wondered if I've failed to communicate the beauty that I feel Catholicism has to offer. I wonder if all the grumblings I had brought home about the Church—grumblings that are a natural part of my role as a religious journalist—had an impact on her. In our household, the scandals of the Church that were thrust in front of the public in the late '90s were old news by then. I had a tendency to tell tales (details and names omitted) of what was happening behind the scenes—churchy gossip that inflates those who indulge in it and at the same time can deflate those hearing it for the first time. On some level, I wondered if I had failed. How traditional of me, I think to myself, who as a true Blue Stater usually lives by the creed of letting people decide vital moral and religious issues in their own way. I always wanted to give my daughter space, and she had taken it.

I always wanted to give my daughter space, and she had taken it.

Yet at the same time I can't help thinking that these are good people at Chestnut Street Church. They study the same Bible, much more intensely than many Catholics. They believe in a Jesus who works in their lives today. You can hear it as they repeat the mantra in that hymn. Jesus is their companion along the way, not an abstract Palestinian prophet in the history books. He is as concerned for them as he was for those who touched his garment and for those he healed back when he walked the earth. It is the kind of Jesus the great mystics in the Catholic tradition know, but relatively few Catholics in the pew feel comfortable talking about, even if they may feel his presence. I wonder, then, if my daughter hasn't managed to find the same divine beauty and power I cherished from Catholicism.

It's a few days before Election Day 2004, and I hear no right-wing politics spewed from the pulpit. Indeed, there is no politics at all. In fact, in my numerous visits to evangelical congregations I rarely hear a political word, the exception being a prayer offered at a Long Island church for our troops in Iraq that bordered on triumphalism. But Chestnut Street provides just pure gospel, pounded home in the usual evangelical style. Not all to my taste—at times like these I'm always looking for Eucharist and quiet reflection to accompany the intense biblical focus and the exuberance. Yet there is something good here. Audrey agrees.

She finds that Chestnut Street, located in a diverse community just south of Elizabeth and gritty New Jersey industrial cities, practices diversity. This is a community where youth are welcome—on this day they have been given the service to pray and preach. The congregation is a mixture of American blacks, Caribbean blacks, Hispanics, and whites. For Audrey, who is biracial, raised in a family with German, Irish, and Caribbean roots, this is the kind of church where she can feel at home. For many of us, especially for those of us in predominantly white churches, diversity is a pleasant add-on at best to social occasions. For others, it is a threat. For Audrey it is who she is, a part of her being, and she seeks it out wherever she is. Including in her faith life.

The Catholic churches where she grew up, both in upstate Albany and Queens, were very homogenous, she tells me. That might surprise pastoral planners who see ethnic diversity as a Catholic trademark. It surprises me, as I had always looked upon those parishes as relatively diverse. Yet Audrey saw them differently. "They were filled mostly with people I couldn't relate to," Audrey says in an impromptu "interview" as we drive back to New York after church. It is the first personal adult conversation we have ever had about faith.

The diversity at Chestnut Street includes a number of factors. The large presence of Hispanics at Chestnut echoes a wider social trend. Some estimates are that as many as half a million Latinos leave the

Catholic Church in the U.S. every year for an evangelical/Pentecostal denomination. This doesn't necessarily indicate that Latinos are becoming more conservative, although evangelical Latinos were far more likely (a 63 percent majority) to vote Republican in the last presidential election than their Catholic neighbors.

But in the evangelical tradition, there is room for women to lead, unlike the all-male priesthood of the Catholic parishes. Among evangelical churches with evangelical outreach, there is almost always a Spanish service. While in many Catholic parishes, it often happens that Spanish-language liturgies are allowed only after a long battle between Anglo parishioners and Latinos. And the emotive character of faith is accepted in many evangelical congregations.

Newsweek notes that younger Latinos are more likely to abandon their Catholic roots. While 72 percent of first-generation Latinos are Catholic, that number goes down to just a bit more than half by the third generation. While Latinos are the fastest growing group among Catholics, they are also the fastest growing group among Mormons, Methodists, and many other denominations. They are changing the Christian religious landscape in America across the board.

Audrey has long had many Latino friends. She has learned Spanish and is comfortable with the ethnic inclusiveness at Chestnut Street. She has many of the concerns about the Catholic Church that many Latino immigrants, as well as other former Catholics who become part of evangelical congregations, share.

The Catholic celibate clergy, she says, makes it difficult for her to believe that they can speak to the needs of family life. She also believes that Catholic teaching on abortion—something she, like many women, opposes but thinks should remain legal—homosexuality, and the status of women is too conservative. She obviously embraces the questions, even if the sign outside her newfound church focuses on answers.

Her view of Catholicism has also been affected by the clergy sex abuse scandal. That abuse, she says, "demonstrated something that is deeply wrong with the Catholic religion." She finds Catholics to be too conservative in their response to the crisis. "Something needs to change, and I can't see Catholics as the type of people who embrace change, even if something is obviously going wrong. The scandals reinforced my reasons for leaving." Audrey has found spiritual succor in this rather conservative evangelical church because she found the church she grew up in to be too rigidly conservative in its views. Something tells me this paradox is not an uncommon one among former Catholics who become evangelicals.

But among young people the conversion traffic between Catholics and evangelicals is not just one-way.

Meet Christopher Cuddy, theology student at the Franciscan University at Steubenville. He's 20 years old, but when you talk to him the names of theologians come tripping off his tongue.

Christopher was raised in a conservative evangelical-style Presbyterian church (Presbyterianism, by the way, is among those Protestant denominations with adherents ranging from the liberal to the strongest conservative evangelicals. They have suffered from doctrinal rifts roughly comparable to the Methodists).

Christopher was raised in Apollo, Pennsylvania, about an hour's drive from Pittsburgh but a world away. It is small-town America. There he was home-schooled through the tenth grade. Other kids in that situation might find themselves absorbed in algebra or geography. Christopher found himself absorbed in God. He spent much of his time studying some hard-core theology.

He would study obscure tracts from the evangelical tradition, exploring themes such as redemption. After high school, he enrolled in Grove City College, a conservative Presbyterian school. His goal was to become a college seminary theology professor.

While Catholic parents sometimes worry that their children might fall into the hands of aggressive evangelical campus groups such as Campus Crusade for Christ, at that Presbyterian school Christopher experienced a different kind of religious approach. For the first time, he began to take Catholicism seriously, particularly the approach embodied by Gabriel Hahn, a fellow freshman.

Gabriel was not from a traditional Catholic background. His religion fermented in an entirely different atmosphere. Gabriel's father is Scott Hahn, a theologian famous in evangelical and some Catholic circles. Now a professor at the Franciscan University at Steubenville, Scott Hahn has written numerous best-selling books and articles chronicling his movement from evangelicalism to Catholicism. His parish lectures around the country fill halls.

"I was looking for an all-encompassing world-view," notes Christopher. He found himself interested in his newfound friend's Catholic faith. It was a startling world, he discovered, a place where he need not fear studies in history and philosophy, areas that were full of caution flags in the evangelical world into which he had immersed himself.

He became enraptured by Catholic metaphors for the Deity. "God is not just a damning King," Christopher discovered as he studied more about Catholicism. "He is first of all a Father." This, combined with a newfound respect for liturgy and the role of hierarchy, both elements he saw reflected in Scripture, brought him to Catholicism.

"God is not just a damning King, He is first of all a Father."

That sacramental life, often taken for granted by cradle Catholics, was a sign to Christopher that God is immersed in the world. "You cannot keep God confined to the walls of the Church," Christopher says.

In the Spring of 2003, while the media was full of accounts of sex abuse perpetrated in the Church, Christopher became a Catholic. He now attends Steubenville, a Catholic college known for its strong emphasis on religious devotion, and one day plans to continue his dream of becoming a seminary or college theology professor, this time from the Catholic tradition.

He sees the Catholic Church as a huge faith family he relishes being a part of. He knows he comes to the Church in a difficult time. Yet, as one imbued in evangelical tradition, he sees the scandals suffered by the Church in the context of Scripture, where God's Chosen People frequently rejected his overtures and lived dissolute immoral lives, only to be called back.

If the Jews of the Bible could have these issues, "it's not a big wonder why the Catholic Church still has problems," says Christopher.

At first, his newfound conversion did not sit well with his parents, James and Debbie Cuddy, and the rest of his family. They had grown to a somewhat grudging acceptance, at least at the time of our interview in the fall of 2004. Christopher, born in an orphanage in Korea, was adopted by his American family.

As always, faith decisions are never just intellectual and doctrinal. They bring the total person into the mix. Christopher has found his niche, and I wish him well as he pursues his Catholic vision. I find myself proud that I am part of a tradition with him that welcomes intellectual inquiry. Welcome to the club, I think, as I hang up the phone after that long conversation with a remarkable young man.

It takes a bit of courage to be a Catholic student at evangelical Northwestern College. Still, the few dozen Catholic students at Northwestern College in Roseville, Minnesota (not to be confused with Northwestern University in Illinois), might very well feel at home, if one looks at the very Catholic architecture of the school located on a scenic lakefront in the suburbs between Minneapolis and St. Paul.

The main building, a former Catholic camp, is bedecked with statues of Mary and the saints. On the day I visited, a large American flag is flown half-staff in honor of the recently deceased Pope John Paul II. It's hard to imagine an evangelical college like this honoring a Catholic prelate in such a way. It certainly would not have happened just a few decades ago.

This school with about 1,600 students, led by Dr. Billy Graham in his younger years, is much like any other college campus on an unusually warm spring day in Minnesota. Students don't look particularly devout as they crowd into the cafeteria. Some of the coeds sport the fashionable belly-baring jeans and tops. There's lots of social banter around circular tables.

But this is different from secular schools or even less-stringent Catholic colleges. Drinking, non-marital sexual activity, and social dancing are prohibited. Prayers are regularly invoked during classes, which heavily focus on theology, liberal arts, and communications.

Ben Brekke, a sophomore graphic design major from Champlin, Minnesota, is comfortable with the easy talk about God on campus. He is a big guy, affable in a teddy bear kind of way. His manner rings of sincerity. Ben has no problems with Northwestern's strict rules, because he said he would follow them even if they were not required of students. In his case, one believes him. There is little apparent guile here. From his mouth, it rings true. He came to Northwestern, he tells me, because he felt that God was calling him here, despite his own Catholic background, a tiny fish represented here in a large sea of evangelicals. Yet while he is comfortable amid the overt Christian religiosity here, he finds that Catholics can have a rough time of it.

He wrote a piece for the college newspaper complaining about what he describes as "denominational discrimination" on campus. When his fellow students discover he is a Catholic, he is often questioned about his beliefs. Some argue, imbued with the apocalyptic thinking prevalent among some evangelicals, that the pope may well be the anti-Christ. It has made him more determined to understand his own Catholic faith, and he is ready with biblically based defense of Catholic Church teaching. He even began organizing a Catholic group on campus, an effort that won both support and opposition from various school administrators.

"In a weird way it has encouraged me to keep up my Catholic faith because I've been bombarded with questions," he says.

Ann McGrath, a junior accounting major from Eagan, Minnesota, says she has gone to bed stewing over remarks in class about Catholicism. She has experienced class prayers for Catholics who are not saved. Yet she finds that once people get to know her on campus, their views of Catholics change. Or at least they are willing to make an exception in her case!

Her parents are glad that she's at Northwestern. But her grandparents worry that the strong evangelical influence will cause her to lose her Catholic faith. She prays regularly with her friends there. Her grandparents might have a point: it's hard to believe that, in this cozy campus filled with attractive and devout evangelicals, bereft of any Catholic support system (not even opportunities to attend Mass), a Catholic belief system could ever be maintained. The statues on the main building overlooking the lake have a lot of heavy lifting to do.

Anna Nussbaum, the University of Notre Dame junior who traveled to Uganda to teach school, grew up where evangelicals dominate—Colorado Springs, Colorado. That medium-sized city is a center for evangelical life. Scores of evangelical organizations, including Focus on the Family and the International Bible Society, have made a home there in the foothills of the Rockies.

While evangelicals often marvel at how Catholics are able to integrate young children into church life—First Communions and Catholic elementary schools are two examples—when teen years arrive, evangelicals almost always have the edge. That's particularly true in places such as Colorado Springs, where they dominate the youth ministry scene.

Catholic youth ministry almost always plays catch-up in such scenarios. The evangelicals have the snazzy music, the tough questions, the ready answers, and emotion-laden services that the confused find comforting. Evangelical services focus on the now, a world very important in the lives of adolescents. Catholic liturgy, still filled with mystery and power, is often weighed down with a long sense of tradition. The Mass might be awe-inspiring for the very young, and comforting to those old enough to make the tradition their own, but for the adolescent it often rings hollow. Catholic parish and diocesan outreach rarely helps either.

> Evangelicals have the snazzy music, the tough questions, the ready answers.

In most places, Confirmation in Catholic parishes is set at junior high age, after which they frequently leave regular Mass attendance only to show up again when they are preparing to get married or baptize a child. Too often, Catholic youth—particularly the majority who attend public schools—are largely left behind in formal programming. The sex abuse scandal hasn't helped. It's not hard to imagine that priests and lay workers in Catholic parishes want to shy away from anything to do with teenagers, lest they rouse suspicion. It's a vacuum only too willingly filled by evangelical youth groups that flourish in growing cities such as Colorado Springs in the West and South.

A study by Christian Smith and Melinda Lundquist Denton titled *Soul Searching: The Religious and Spiritual Lives of American Teenagers* (Oxford University Press) confirms this anecdotal observation about how Catholic adolescents relate to their church.

In their study, they note that Catholic young people "stand out among the U.S. Christian teenagers as consistently scoring lower on most measures of religiosity." Catholic youth, they said, are less inclined to believe in a personal God and to have had an intense spiritual experience in their lives.

But not so with evangelicals, as Anna Nussbaum can attest. She was confronted on her plane to Africa with the question, "Are you saved?" It was a question she had heard many times before as evangelical youth leaders would pester her in her high school years.

As we saw, her standard response was: "I'm

Catholic." The standard rebuttal would be: "That's not good enough. Are you saved?"

It wore her down enough that, in what she describes as a rebellious youth phase, Anna began attending an Assemblies of God youth group. The joyful and friendly atmosphere, complete with rock bands and other elements of youth culture, had her hooked. But beneath the joyful Christian revelry, she found that the group was very anti-Catholic. It bothered her enough that she quit and returned to her Catholic practice.

She found that as she learned more about Catholicism, she discovered that it was open to intellectual inquiry in ways that evangelicals often were not. It is an irony, she says, that a Church with so many bedrock doctrines provides more intellectual freedom than a tradition which has always prided itself on the individual believer coming to a decision before God. It's that tradition of intellectual Catholicism she has decided to study at Notre Dame, where she is a Great Books major and a theology minor. She has the intellectual tools—both in Church history and Scripture—to provide answers. In that sense, she is rare indeed among her young adult Catholic peers.

If Kathy Swistock were to check a form under

"religion" she might be filling in "Catholic" or "evangelical." Much depends on when and where you reach her. Whatever the box on the form, you can count on Kathy taking her Christian faith seriously, no matter the denominational label.

The Ashburn, Virginia, woman, 45, was raised Catholic but admits it meant little to her as a child. As a young woman she encountered a non-denominational evangelical group, underwent a born-again experience, and then joined a Presbyterian church as the best way to manifest that newfound Christian commitment.

Then she met her husband, Christopher, also raised an indifferent Catholic who rediscovered Christianity while getting involved in a Campus Crusade for Christ evangelical group while attending college. They bonded and, to keep peace in the extended family, planned for a Catholic wedding.

Then Kathy discovered the attitudes of many of her evangelical friends were not well disposed to her warming to Catholicism. Many boycotted the wedding. The elders in her Presbyterian church were aghast, upset that one of their new bright and shining members should allow the Church of Rome to consecrate her marriage.

Fast-forward 20 years. The couple now have five children, ages 7 through 18. After years of staying away from church, Kathy rediscovered her Catholicism and formally rejoined the Catholic Church in 1995. She credits Catholic schools for her newfound involvement; while her husband has mixed views about the Church, as a military child growing up he found that the brothers at the Catholic school he attended in Guam encouraged him the most. At the time she rejoined the Church, she was coping with a personal crisis, and found that it was Catholic spirituality that made the most sense to her.

"I had a complete change of prayer life," she recalls. Some have said that Catholicism is the Hinduism of Christianity, a religious system where there are so many varied spiritualities. While there is a popular perception that Catholics march in lockstep under a demanding and stern pope, the reality is that Catholics find a variety of ways to connect with God, from Dorothy Day's Catholic Worker and its physical outreach to the poor to ancient spiritualities promoted by religious orders such as the Spiritual Exercises of St. Ignatius, so closely associated with the Jesuit community. Kathy found her niche in Carmelite spirituality, a charism focused on contemplating suffering that owes much to the writings of mystics such as Teresa of Avila and John of the Cross. That hard-boiled, old-world, Spanish spirituality resonated with her. It is a spirituality that talks frequently about the dark night of the soul, that moment of despair necessary before spiritual insight and the love of God can enter into a troubled person. "It helped me cope at a difficult time," Kathy says.

Just like when she encountered evangelicalism, Kathy immersed herself in her newfound Catholicism. She took classes, read all she could, and found herself able to defend the Church against the onslaughts of her evangelical friends, even at the height of the priest sex abuse crisis. A priest told her something that she considers wise about how to approach any Christian doctrine or spirituality: "If it doesn't lead you to Jesus, just let it drop." She began to appreciate that many of the roads paved by Catholicism led her more deeply into the gospel, rather than the worship of hierarchy her old evangelical friends had warned her about.

Yet this is not a Happily-Ever-After story. Kathy is still torn. She now attends an evangelical church with her family. Her husband, for years indifferent to religious faith, found himself attracted to a Sovereign

Grace Ministries congregation in town. Kathy, a believer that the Scriptures teach that the husband should be the head of the family, now goes to the local evangelical church, providing the family a unified front. Still, she admits, she will occasionally go off to Catholic confession for spiritual solace. She is among the growing number of Americans who mix-and-match denominations.

As one who has lived on those boundaries between evangelicalism and Catholicism, Kathy sees strengths in both approaches. Small evangelical churches have a stronger sense of the social community, even if their theology focuses on the individual believer and his/her relationship with Jesus. She finds the mass of Catholics indifferent to what she found as startling doctrinal beliefs, such as the doctrine that Jesus is truly present at the Eucharist or church teaching against contraception, something that she and her husband argue about regularly. (It is interesting that in some evangelical circles strict Catholic teachings on sexual concerns, unpopular among many Catholics themselves, have made inroads. W. Bradford Wilcox, writing in *Touchstone* magazine, suggests that evangelicals need to take heed of Pope Paul VI's *Humanae Vitae*, the encyclical that described why the Church forbids contraception. He also argues that evangelicals should, like Catholics, be more strict about divorce and remarriage. Wilcox, a sociologist at the University of Virginia, insists that family stability is not only religiously prescribed—it is also good social policy because committed married couples are better equipped to avoid poverty and are better able to raise children effectively.)

Kathy's evangelical friends, she says, focus on "a personal relationship with Jesus." They do good works, "not because you are a good person, but because you are doing it for the love of Him."

Kathy finds that evangelicals are impatient at times. Pressure is forced on people to make a decision at this very moment for Christ. By contrast, "Catholics see it as a life's journey, with a series of conversion experiences." Her own life has told Kathy that the model of the lifetime journey is a metaphor that resonates most deeply with her. It is a journey she knows is not yet complete. It will not end with a single commitment to follow Jesus. It is a commitment that affirms itself day after day.

Barbara Baker, 43, a Cincinnati Catholic woman married to an evangelical Christian for the past 14 years, suggests that it is important to talk out religious themes before marriage. She and her husband, Bert, 48, regularly speak to marriage preparation couples in programs sponsored by the Catholic Archdiocese of Cincinnati.

With their six-year-old son, Carl, the couple have long Sundays. They routinely attend both services at an American Baptist congregation and Catholic Mass. Their son attends Catholic religious education.

Barbara is a proponent of "the domestic church," the spiritual life of her family together.

Barbara is a proponent of what she calls "the domestic church," the spiritual life of her family together. She says that she was attracted to her husband because, not despite of, his serious religious commitment. Unlike others in their situation, she never considered converting her husband.

There are difficulties. She is upset at times that her husband cannot receive Communion with her. But she's learned from her evangelical contacts. She wishes that Catholics were more vocal about their faith and willing to share it with others, the way evangelicals routinely do. When she talks with couples contemplating what are called ecumenical marriages, she and her husband offer an example that such relationships can work. It is in such marriages that the evangelical-Catholic bond is being lived out most concretely. While institutional church structures may have difficulty incorporating them, couples such as the Bakers have found spiritual solace in their domestic church, respecting and relishing differences while praying together with a common Christian heritage.

I ran across Mary Jane Ballou, now involved in the real estate trade in Florida, when she was head of the library at the American Bible Society.

I have great affection for librarians (I am married to one). Organizations blessed to have librarians should appreciate them. They have a credo of service. They are also invariably well read and knowledgeable. And, because they come from a profession that is largely low paid, they are like a modern monastic order dedicated to the pursuit of knowledge while the rest of us pursue more mercenary ends. They also tend to know where the best affordable restaurants are in any town.

Mary Jane was no exception. She and I would have occasional talks at the Bible Society. We were both Catholic, relatively small fish in a sea of evangelicals. Mary Jane, raised in a variety of denominations, embraced Catholicism at an older age. Her Catholicism is a brand particularly rooted in tradition. Thanks to our shared interest in a Catholic blog led by author Amy Welborn, we made contact, and I told her about my project. She was eager to talk about her experiences with evangelicals and was quick to note that both religious groups are learning from each other. She sees examples both in her American Bible Society experience and in Gainesville, Florida, the college town in the northern part of the state.

At the Bible Society, she found that evangelicals and Catholics who worked together often spoke a different language. For example, the very word "evangelizing" meant very different things to both groups.

To many Catholics and mainstream Protestants, evangelizing is a long-term process. It's not unusual, for instance, for Catholic missionary orders in countries seemingly immune to heavy Christian influence, such as Japan, to serve in education and health fields as ways to gain the long-term trust of people. The goal is to make a permanent mark on the wider culture, knowing that conversion may well come, or not, in God's time. Yet for evangelicals, conversion demands immediate and quick commitment, a substantial change and conversion.

"Evangelicals could not understand how you could have the Bible not affect someone practically," said Mary Jane, noting that at the Bible Society, various schemes were put forth to present the Bible in such a way that it would generate conversions. While the organization hired Catholics, "they didn't want to hear what Catholics had to say," particularly when it came to the meaning of conversion.

Studies would be commissioned to find out how Catholics related to the Bible. Eventually, a Catholic leader would be located who reflected a more evangelical view of conversion and the Scriptures. But, noted Mary Jane, that was just a small slice of the giant picture of Catholicism.

Prayer styles were different as well. Prayer at the Bible Society was encouraged. Catholics, used to a prayer with more universal themes, would be surprised with evangelical prayers directed at the particular issue at hand, usually involving the meeting that was about to happen. God would be invoked to intervene in a difficult personnel issue or a financial crisis. Catholics, noted Mary Jane, often found such prayers presumptuous, as if God didn't have more important business to take care of somewhere else in the world.

Mary Jane, who once studied for a doctorate in American religious history, noted how evangelicals in the organization looked at financial concerns with a residue of historic Calvinism, the belief that prosperity was an indication of God's favor. Catholic theology, which often talks about God having a preferential option for the poor, looks at wealth differently. Even when prayer for the sick was offered, Catholics and evangelicals did it differently. It is not uncommon for Catholics to pray for a severely ill person to have a happy death. Such prayers are rarely heard in evangelical circles. I can remember a number of times when God was invoked for a physical healing of a sick Bible Society worker or loved one. I always wondered if the thought crept in that God had failed when the health of the person being prayed for had a setback.

Always the astute observer, particularly of things religious, Mary Jane is quick to observe how

Catholics in the heavily evangelical region of north Florida have been influenced by their neighbors. That section of Florida is more like the old Confederacy than southern Florida, where the region around Miami is swamped with former New Yorkers and immigrants from Latin American and the Caribbean. Mary Jane, whose religious quest has brought her all across the religious spectrum, from various Protestant denominations, to Russian Orthodox and now Roman Catholicism, explained how Catholic parishes mimic their evangelical neighbors in her section of north Florida.

Priests don't just preside over a ritual at Sunday Mass. They banter, sometimes about the fortunes of the Florida Seminoles football team. The personality of the prayer leader counts for more than it does in regions such as the Northeast, where Catholics are the dominant players in the Christian marketplace.

In Bible Belt-influenced areas such as north Florida, Catholic parishes don't just offer the sacraments. In a region that is growing exponentially, parishes offer small groups and support for every possible need. Various social ills—overeating and alcoholism, for example—are provided for by support groups. Various demographics—mothers with small children, for one—can come to the church and find social support. For Mary Jane, it's a therapeutic model of church, not so much focused on the sacramental role. And, like their evangelical neighbors, Catholic parishes are large and fill the churches each Sunday. Religion is important in the Bible Belt, for both Catholics and evangelicals.

Overt enthusiasm, not quiet pietism, is emphasized. At one local parish, the priest will offer a call-and-response litany.

"God is good!" he says.

"All the time!" shouts the congregation.

Of course, that's the kind of practice borrowed from evangelicals. It is not in the Catholic rubrics for the Mass. Some might call it innovative pastoral practice, but Mary Jane, for one, is not pleased. In particular she finds the model of parish-as-therapeutic-support-center to be an alien concept.

"That's not for me. I could get that at the self-help aisle at Barnes & Noble," she says, protesting what she sees as a more personality-driven Catholic liturgy. Yet, she realizes, in an atmosphere permeated with evangelical practices, with thousands of new families coming to Florida seeking out religious experiences and community, it is a losing battle. Catholic churches in the Bible Belt will continue to invoke many of the cultural traditions of evangelical-minded Americans, much like missionaries in Africa incorporate the sounds of native drums into the sacred liturgy. The growth of the church depends upon acceding to, even celebrating, the cultural demands and expectations of the locals.

"That [kind of liturgy] is not for me—I could get that at the self-help aisle at Barnes & Noble."

An article in the February 14, 2005 issue of *Time* put a mainstream media imprimatur on Mary Jane's observations. Tim Padgett, the author, notes that St. Mark's Church in Charlotte, North Carolina, has 2,800 families, many of them transplants from the North. They hear a rock music band at Sunday Mass, much like those heard in the evangelical churches that are at the center of Bible Belt life. The Catholic population in Charlotte is growing by 10 percent a year, a far cry from the empty pews now common in the Northeast and Midwest. In all, the South saw a rise in the number of Catholics at almost 30 percent in the 1990s, three times higher than that experienced by Baptists. A priest I knew who resettled in Charlotte after serving in urban Dayton, Ohio, said he felt renewed doing ministry in a region that was growing in the numbers of Catholics, versus places in the Northeast and Midwest which, while still filled with Catholics, have experienced a noticeable decline in numbers over the past few decades.

Catholicism in the South "is changing the nature of the church in America," says Patrick McHenry, a Republican congressman from Charlotte and a Catholic quoted in *Time*. In the Bible Belt, influenced by their evangelical neighbors, Catholics are flourishing because, while they take on the innovative marketing and cultural accoutrements of the South, they are particularly orthodox in their beliefs, says McHenry.

While some church leaders see this growth as affirming, others are cautious. Father Kevin Wildes, S.J., president of Loyola University in New Orleans, a school that includes a center for the study of Catholics in the South, wonders whether Catholics in the Bible Belt might get swallowed up by the wider culture. Given a few generations, could there be much discernible difference between Catholics in the South and their evangelical neighbors?

"The question is whether Catholicism in the South simply becomes another form of evangelical Fundamentalism with incense," Father Wildes told *Time*.

6

Catholic priest,
top evangelical

*"I don't remember it well because
I was two weeks old."*

Rev. Richard Neuhaus, pointing to the moment of his
baptism as the time he was saved

Walk into the offices of *First Things*, a religion journal of opinion based in Manhattan, and one is struck by the photos of luminaries, many of the avatars of American conservatism. There is Supreme Court Justice Clarence Thomas. On another wall is one of Michael Novak, Catholic theologian and passionate free market advocate. He is joined by Cardinals Avery Dulles and Joseph Ratzinger (now Pope Benedict XVI) and, of course, William F. Buckley.

They are all linked with photos of Father Richard Neuhaus, the founder and guiding spirit of *First Things*.

Father Neuhaus is a former Lutheran pastor who, after writing a book called *The Catholic Moment*, about why Catholics are prime players in American politics and cultural life, decided to become part of that moment. He was ordained a priest for the Archdiocese of New York and has maintained offices here, where he writes scathing missives attacking abortion and gay rights, among other things. His back section ramblings on all sorts of subjects regularly illustrate an engrossed mind skewering the ideas of the liberal religious world he was once a part of in the 1960s.

Father Neuhaus was a liberal activist, opposed

to the Vietnam War and a co-founder of a group called Clergy and Laity Concerned. As he moved to the right of the political spectrum and to the center of Catholic life, he has found himself allied with conservative evangelicals on many issues. He and Chuck Colson, the former Nixon aide who went to jail for Watergate-related crimes and emerged as a fervent proponent of prison reform and Christianity, cobbled together a statement that argued that Catholics and evangelicals, while they remain theologically different, have much to work together on transforming American culture in a way that reflects the moral values of both groups.

According to Neuhaus each group is, in many ways, becoming much like the other.

"Catholics are always in the process of becoming more American," he says, tracing the story of Catholics in this country. "America is a Protestant culture and evangelicalism is the dominant form of Protestantism."

At the same time, evangelicals are quietly borrowing elements of Catholic culture and belief as well. Mark Noll, in the *Scandal of the Evangelical Mind*, argues that his fellow evangelicals need to take more seriously the study of culture, an aspect of religion that has always been central to Catholicism, with its long tradition of scholarship and art.

Evangelicals are also taking seriously biblical scholarship, natural law teaching, and respect for Christian tradition, aspects that they share with Catholicism. What is more important, however, says Neuhaus, is that meetings between evangelical scholars and Catholic leaders have begun to change the dynamic of religious life in the United States. Tradition-minded Catholics and evangelicals are discovering that they share in the pre-Reformation formulations of faith, such as belief in the divinity of Jesus, that shape historic Christianity. Such shared core beliefs are grounds for theological dialogue. After Vatican II, it was thought that the most fruitful realm of ecumenical dialogue would be among Catholics, Anglicans, and Lutherans, because of their shared sacramental tradition. But, says Neuhaus, liberal mainstream Protestantism has lost its way and is unable or unwilling to articulate basic Christian truths. Arguments over women clergy (The Anglicans and many Lutheran denominations ordain women) or sexual issues haven't helped. The end result: it's Catholics and evangelicals who are forging close bonds, particularly among conservative activists.

Those long arguments dating from the Reformation, which shaped the views of Protestants about their Catholic neighbors in the U.S., are coming to an end. This is true at least in most respectable evangelical circles. But if you want to find old-fashioned evangelical anti-Catholicism, it isn't difficult. "A major change that has filtered down is that being anti-Catholic is not a constitutive part of being evangelical," says Father Neuhaus. And Catholics and evangelicals are beginning to share a language to describe how their views of theological concerns are closer than traditionally thought.

It's not to say that all is placid on the evangelical/Catholic ecumenical front. When, as noted earlier, Father Neuhaus and evangelical Chuck Colson, along with other religious leaders, put together a joint statement in 1994 emphasizing what unites Catholics and evangelicals the event was barely noted in the Catholic press or in the Catholic pews.

But in the evangelical world Colson felt the heat. "I began getting hate mail. I had people telling me I was a heretic," he told National Public Radio. That statement, he said, cost his famous ministry to prisoners about a million dollars in donations from anti-Catholic evangelicals.

Father Neuhaus knows about that personal suspicion among some evangelicals that Catholics are second-rate Christians, not really saved. Father Neuhaus, a regular at ecumenical gatherings, knows what it's liked to be asked questions such as "Are you saved?" He has a ready answer, pointing to the time of his baptism in a Lutheran church, although he adds, "I don't remember it too well because I was two weeks old."

That, he knows, puzzles more fervent evangelicals, who invariably point to a particular point in their conscious life when they made the decision to follow Jesus (they almost always use his first name). "All the rest of my life has been growing up in the sense of baptismal regeneration," he says. But Father Neuhaus agrees that the born-again experience is something, cited in John 3, available to all Christians, whether they carry the evangelical tag or not.

"It's possible and even desirable that one has a reality of reawakening . . . In that sense we can say that we are to be born again."

Still, the evangelical certitude on things religious is at the least befuddling to non-evangelicals, even conservative ones.

Father Neuhaus, one of the rare Catholic priests

who is a regular at evangelical events, hears the witnessing. And, he adds, "If you wanted to be unsympathetic," the constant resort to witnessing, usually featuring some perfidious deed that is now fully repented for in light of a new life in Christ, could be heard as boasting and spiritual egotism. Still, it has a long history, coming out of nineteenth-century revivalism. Father Neuhaus sees it as one strain of Christian spirituality.

Many secularists find spiritual certitude, the evangelical sense that there is right and wrong, annoying.

Many secularists find this kind of spiritual certitude, the evangelical sense that there is right and wrong, annoying. Father Neuhaus has his own theory as to why blue state liberals are confounded by evangelical rhetoric.

"Most people want to do what they want to do," he says. "We live in a libertine and licentious culture, all in the name of freedom." While conservative evangelicals have their certitudes, so do liberals as well, says Father Neuhaus.

"It's pretty much of a tossup," he says, describing the difference between the degree of open-mindedness of students and faculty at places he has lectured, such as Yale, with its secular liberal tradition, and various southern evangelical divinity schools.

Devout blue staters such as *New York Times* columnist Frank Rich see evangelicals as amassing huge power. After all, they have been credited with electing a president. Their views about what is and what is not appropriate are, it is said, beginning to stifle Hollywood's creative freedom. On the other hand, evangelicals themselves still feel uncomfortable, even if the media proclaims that they control two-thirds of the federal government—Congress and the presidency—and are working on taking over the third, the judiciary. Outsiders view evangelical conservatives as arrogant seekers of power. For whatever reason, evangelicals don't feel the power. They are as likely to complain about being persecuted as they are gloating about some perceived political triumph. They are more likely to be intellectually humble and searching. "They know they are the outsiders, that they are looked down upon," says Father Neuhaus. Perhaps that is why we hear so much these days about conservative evangelicals' strident complaints about religious "persecution," particularly when prayers are denied at public events or they appear to be on the losing side of a church/state conflict.

And like many who are uncomfortable with their status, they can sometimes come across as arrogant and unyielding when pressured or threatened. Perhaps that defiant "red state" attitude so looked down upon by the intelligentsia—personified in the frequent political rants of Jerry Falwell or Pat Robertson—is at its root caused by an uneasy status, a sense that evangelicals may be emerging into the political mainstream but are at heart still in the cultural and intellectual backwaters.

The growing alliance between evangelicals and conservative Catholics is evident in one startling item, rarely remarked about at the time. Father Neuhaus is certainly not an evangelical-style, glad-handing preacher, and maintains a kind of austereness stereotypical of his Lutheran ministry roots. He has publicly described evangelical worship music as banal and uninteresting. Still, when *Time* selected its 50 most influential evangelical leaders in early 2005, Father Neuhaus was among them. A Catholic priest being selected as an evangelical leader raised few eyebrows—just one indication of how relations between evangelicals and Catholics, particularly conservative Catholics, are evolving and even been taken for granted.

While they may be accepting of Catholic priests who support their political agenda, conservative evangelicals have certainly not lost their zeal for conversion. Evangelicals can still make converts out of Catholics imbued with a sophisticated education and cosmopolitan worldview. In our next chapter we will meet a brother and sister who, raised in a traditional Catholicism, have embraced an evangelical-style Christian witness.

The O'Haras

"My life sucked. Then I read the Bible. Now my life doesn't suck so much."

A somewhat jaded worker in an evangelical publishing house, explaining the basic outline of the conversion stories featured in the group's publications

John O'Hara was imbued with a traditional Irish-Catholic spirituality. For him, God was a real presence. A salesman, he was in a business where nothing was guaranteed. He was only as good as his last sale. Every stab at a commission that was successfully completed was evidence that God answered prayers.

He went to Mass every day. Some said he looked like a priest. Yet he realized that he wasn't perfect. John battled alcoholism. His marriage was rocky. There were periods of absence from his wife and children. Faith and good practice were a struggle, to be won through the regular readings of the great Catholic classics such as *The Imitation of Christ*. Nothing came easy in John O'Hara's life or his demanding piety.

When he died in 1970 he left a void in the life of his youngest, Cathy O'Hara, then an eighth grader at St. Anne's School in Garden City, Long Island. He also left her a faith in the belief that God answers prayers, even in the most difficult of struggles.

Cathy and I were in the same grade together, sharing eight years of intense confinement that only parochial schools in the booming post-war New York suburbs could engender. We were packed, 40–45 to a class, reflecting the sheer numbers of Catholic children who made the postwar suburbs such vibrant places. The school was operated by the Religious of the Sacred Heart of Mary, an order that ran sophisticated all-women's institutions around the world, including Marymount in Manhattan. St. Anne's was one of their few parish elementary schools, and they brought to it a sophistication and worldliness that few other orders did. Many of us felt that they opened a world to us beyond our enclosed suburban communities. Graduates included New York mayor Rudolph Guiliani and Bill Donohue, the firebrand who reinvigorated the Catholic League for Religious and Civil Rights. My graduating class boasts doctors, a network newscaster, and at least two social activists who became deeply involved in the Maryknoll effort in Latin America.

Cathy was perhaps the most popular of the girls in that class, intelligent and quick with a smile and a kind word. Everyone in that class, a tightknit crew, thought we knew everything about each other. Yet Cathy's ease and sociability masked a struggle that not all were privy to. Her parents were divorced, a rarity in those days among post-war Catholics. Growing up in a section of Long Island considered comfortably middle-class if not affluent, the Garden

City-Floral Park-New Hyde Park sections, the O'Haras struggled financially, more than the rest of us who were confident that their fathers' jobs, invariably in the city and dependent upon the Long Island Railroad, would remain steady and able to maintain a middle-class lifestyle.

After a similar dose of Catholic upbringing and education, our respective spiritual journeys took different paths. Cathy now lives in Princeton, New Jersey, where she is a Spanish teacher at a local Catholic academy. Divorced, she is the mother of two teenagers, Clare and Lizzie. Together they attend an evangelical church, an anomaly in the secular swirl of college town and genteel Ivy League institutions.

While now an evangelical, Cathy is unwilling to utter a disdainful reference to her own Catholic background. "People were kind," she recalled of her early parochial school days, when the nuns overlooked occasional late tuition payments and quietly looked out for her well-being. There were, of course, the occasional bouts of Catholic school oddities. We recalled a certain math teacher, beset by emotional problems and besieged by overactive junior-high classes, who stopped algebra and had us recite the Rosary. We certainly got familiar with the holy mysteries, but few of us became calculus scholars.

She learned early on from her parents that church was important, prayer wasn't silly, and that "there was a God who cared for us." She learned from her father's traditional Catholic piety that "there was a personal God in heaven who cared about our hurts." God was never seen as austere and far away.

And then, after her father died, much of her faith life was put on the shelf. She moved to the Rockaway section of Queens and lived under the supervision of her older brothers. She attended a local Catholic girls' academy where the religion curriculum, the outgrowth of the turbulent '70s in the Church, eschewed hard doctrines and theology for seminars on interpersonal relationships.

"We would bullsh—," she says now, adding "the whole thing was puffery, real loosey-goosey." Growing up in a difficult family situation, Cathy admits she was seeking some strong rules. She didn't get it in her high school religion class at the time.

"At that point everything was gray, and everything was uncertain," she recalls.

While she continued to go to Mass through high

school, after she went off to college at SUNY Albany, she abandoned formal religious practice.

Cathy became reacquainted with her Catholic faith through various influences. A year in Spain brought her back to attending Mass. She met a Mexican priest in Rome, who was invited to stay with her family in Queens. He told her, "you have a faith, you have to find it again," and he offered to pray for her and her brother Sean. He left her a Spanish New Testament, and she began to pour through its contents.

Sean, a bit older than Cathy, was then going through a severe decline. He was drinking excessively and had difficulty holding on to work. After hitting what the alcohol experts call rock bottom, he got sober and began attending Alcoholics Anonymous. That group's call for a higher power intrigued Sean, and he became more and more interested in Christian faith. He became the family's "Jesus freak" and began attending services at a Manhattan evangelical church. One day, while on a walk on the beach in Rockaway, he challenged his sister to accept Jesus. And she did.

Cathy sees her own salvation as complete, something she felt her father never was comfortable with. His Catholic piety was a daily struggle. Now, she says, her personal salvation "is a completed act. I don't have to hope for it each day." Life has not been easy for her since; she has been through a divorce, difficult financial times, and the normal struggles of raising headstrong girls. But there is a serenity that committed Christians have, and Cathy radiates that.

She feels that the Word preached at her church is something she learns from and grows with everyday. It has helped her immeasurably, she says, as she searches through the wide evangelical world for the Bible studies and preaching that she believes will make her a better Christian.

These days Cathy is a proud evangelical, but she still maintains a Catholic sensibility in many ways. If she were to attend a wedding, she would want the service to be at her evangelical church. But the reception afterwards, she says, she'd want to have at a Catholic social hall.

> Though a proud evangelical, Cathy maintains a Catholic sensibility in many ways.

Cathy attributes her own conversion to her brother Sean's efforts. That's not surprising, since she's not the only person Sean has challenged to accept Jesus—Sean spends his working career trying to convert others.

The Reverend Sean is pastor of young adults and outreach at a midtown Manhattan evangelical church, a landmark in midtown Manhattan. I met him at the little coffee shop he runs as an outreach for the church.

It is a rainy day, mild for early December in New York. Already the Christmas crowds are starting to clog the sidewalks on West 57th Street, just down the block from Carnegie Hall. This is the capital of blue state territory, where people are usually secular, Catholic, or Jewish. Sean's approach is casual and non-threatening. Sean is not the fire-and-brimstone type, and surely that approach wouldn't work on these streets anyway.

Across the street is a Starbucks, where coffee can go for more than $5 a cup. Here it's free, an unheard of bargain in New York. Cookies are also available free of charge. The music is not the usual ponderous Christian rock or gospel usually heard around evangelical outreach circles. This afternoon the sounds of the Beatles' "Yellow Submarine" play over the loudspeaker. Still, only about half the tables are occupied, an indication that jaded New Yorkers are reluctant to drop in on a bargain if the price might include some preaching.

The coffee shop outreach began after September 11. New Yorkers, noted Sean, were seeking out the church as a place to meditate in the middle of the day after the catastrophe. It is, ironically, a very Catholic belief that churches should be set aside for particular shrines for prayer. Sean acknowledges that most evangelicals emphasize that prayer can happen everywhere. But like St. Paul, he is willing to work with the local customs.

Sean, who I haven't seen in more than 35 years, I still recognize when I see him. He wears his hair in a shaggy, '60s kind of way. He is past 50, but there are only specks of gray and no signs of thinning on top.

"I want people to come over and feel comfortable," says Sean. When people are comfortable, he says, they will approach him about religious and personal issues. And it happens frequently. Just recently, he noted, he talked with a lesbian woman who was seeking counseling. His approach, while consistent with much evangelical teaching, would not be comforting to many gay activists or even most cosmopolitan New Yorkers who pride themselves on tolerance and acceptance of various lifestyles. "We welcome gay people but we do not welcome gay sin," he says, promoting an abstinence approach to gay sexuality consistent with most evangelical beliefs and the official position of the Catholic Church.

"Who is a Christian?," I ask him. Does he believe that the only ones who can be categorized as Christians are those who have undergone a born-again experience as cited in John 3? I tell him that many evangelicals can make Catholics like me—and most of Sean's own family—feel apart, not up to grade.

He uses the metaphor of marriage. "If you say you are married, you are. It happens when you go to the altar and say 'I do'," he says. Evangelicals believe in that personal experience of an adult faith galvanized by a commitment to follow Jesus. "It's more than just anyone going to a house of worship that's not a synagogue or a mosque," says Sean.

He points to his own conversion. In true evangelical fashion, he is quite specific. It has a date, October 24, 1979, when he made his own altar call. But the roots of that call, he says, go back to his own Catholic upbringing.

As a little boy, he recalls, a nun at St. Anne's School had her second-graders close their eyes and imagine themselves at Golgotha, where Jesus was crucified. Sean remembers it as an intense religious experience, surpassing his own participation in the Catholic sacraments and other religious observances. Putting yourself into the Gospel scene is an old Jesuit practice. This nun was willing to use it with second-graders; it's a shame it is not invoked more for adult Catholics. In Sean's case, it was highly effective and memorable.

"She painted the picture," he says. "She said 'He's done this for you.' She made it personal."

After going through a 12-step program to deal with his alcoholism, he explored the famous Third Step: turning one's life over to God as we understand Him. Jimmy Carter was in the White House, and Sean devoured articles in *Time* and other popular publications to explore what the "born again" phenomenon was all about. His faith search brought him to seminary, where he is still studying, between work at the church and tending to the needs of his family, including wife Beverly and their two teenage children. They live in Queens.

His marriage and family life, it would appear, would seem to have an impact on his preaching. Beverly is African American. They met at church.

It is something we have in common. Both of us, raised as middle-class white guys from largely Irish backgrounds in the Long Island suburbs, have discovered that inter-racial marriage has thrust us into an awareness of civil rights issues we surely never would have had otherwise.

Flash forward to February. Sean has been given the preaching assignment while his pastor has taken a week off. It's Black History Month, and Sean's impassioned talk is linked to Martin Luther King's dream speech and the Greensboro sit-ins of the 1960s.

The service is very traditional Protestant. The music, enhanced by professionals who have trained at Julliard, fills the packed sanctuary. There are few modern accommodations here: the people use hymnals and Bibles, much like they have since the Reformation. No flashy Power Point screens here. It has a churchy feel, unlike the shopping-mall look of many new evangelical congregations that flourish in growing suburbs and exurbs around the country. This is old-time religion.

But this church has changed considerably over the years. It is part of church lore that an elder back in the '60s proclaimed that that church—once a bastion of oldtime Protestant New York—would be integrated over his dead body. He died within a week. Now the church has a large African American, Caribbean, and Hispanic base who come to services from all over the city.

Sean's preaching is shaped by his New York roots. His accent, and references, ring differently from the southern style most are accustomed to when they hear evangelical preaching. When he healed a woman with an affliction who touched his garment, Jesus, he says, was surrounded by crowds, "like an F-train at rush hour" or, "seventh inning at Yankee Stadium." Like the civil rights crusaders, we are all struggling and need to draw upon faith in Him, emphasizes Sean. It is a message greeted positively, like most evangelical preaching geared towards average people struggling with difficult concerns. This is down-home, not bookish, theology.

Yet Sean still considers himself shaped in many ways by his Irish-Catholic background. On that day in the church coffee shop, he credited the Catholic Church for its ongoing and strong stand against abortion. He reflects the growing political/cultural consensus developing between evangelicals and conservative Catholics cited by Father Neuhaus and what I've seen in demonstrations against abortion. During the arguments in the early '90s over an ongoing gay curriculum in the New York City public schools, Sean joined a coalition that brought together evangelicals and Catholics opposed to various sex education efforts in the city public schools.

Those were the days when the city's tabloids were filled with arguments about condom education and the famous child's book *Heather Has Two Mommies*, which suggested that homosexual and heterosexual couples were equally equipped to raise children. It was a revolt that surprised many, including the editorial writers of the *New York Times*, who had no idea that such a coalition could galvanize New York's outer boroughs. Those sorts of disputes happened in Kansas or Alabama, it was thought, and not cosmopolitan New York. Still, parents in Queens and other places jammed auditoriums and demanded that local school boards abandon the gay rights education project. The argument eventually resulted in the ouster of a New York City school chancellor.

Those sorts of disputes happened in Kansas or Alabama, it was thought, and not cosmopolitan New York.

What Sean realizes, and many of New York's media elite who rarely venture outside of Manhattan don't, is that the religious landscape of the city has become more evangelical in the past few decades. A February 2005 article in the *Wall*

Street Journal notes that the face of evangelicalism in the U.S. is as likely to be brown, black or yellow and urban as it is to be the stereotypical white rural southerner or midwesterner.

The *Journal* estimates that nearly a third of evangelicals are Asian, African, Latin American, or Pacific Islanders. Whole evangelical institutions, such as the Westminster Theological Seminary in Pennsylvania, with its outreach focus to Korean Americans, are dedicated to reaching new immigrants. When my neighborhood Korean dry cleaner in Queens found out a few years ago that I worked for the American Bible Society, she uninhibitedly asked what my favorite Scripture story was—an unusual discussion during an American business transaction. When I brought her a copy of the Bible in Korean, she beamed.

The times, and the *Times*, have changed. While blindsided by the exertion of evangelical political power in the schools' controversies of the early '90s, the *New York Times* has begun to discover and report about the growth of evangelicals, particularly in the outer boroughs. Their churches have become the center of protest against same-sex marriage and other cultural issues, while at the same time retaining their liberal support for housing and job initiatives. These are people more likely to vote Republican in what remains a solid Democratic region.

Sean sees it as a triumph of a coalition between evangelicals and Catholics who agree on social issues. "They were like my uncles," he said about much of the leadership of the coalition against the acceptance of homosexuality in the public schools. While evangelical pastors have been in the forefront, they were joined by Irish-Catholics imbued with a traditional sense of morality and what was appropriate for children. That cultural reticence about what is appropriate in sexual matters creates a deep bond between tradition-minded Catholics and evangelicals, particularly those like Sean who have lived in both worlds. If this nation is seeking a more restrained sexual ethic, it will find its basis in the Catholic and evangelical worldview embodied by activist Christians such as Reverend Sean.

Holy Land revisited

It's been a year, and I'm back in the hot late-May sun at Holy Land in Orlando.

My wife and friends wonder if I have a screw loose. No self-respecting liberal-thinking northeasterner would venture into such a strange world, a place where the worldviews of Disney and Jimmy Swaggart intersect. The 10-year-old daughter of a Catholic friend of mine sees it as sacrilegious to combine the sacred and the profane in a Holy Land amusement park. But I want to find out if what I've learned about American religion today is reflected in what I see amid the exhibits and shows at this unlikely site just off Route 4. I am alone.

After three days attending the Catholic Press Association convention in Disney, I am tired of the "Have a Magic Day" I hear repeated robotically by the employees of the Mouse. Through it all, I am determined to have the kind of day I want to have, not what is pre-determined for me by corporate entertainment chiefs. I faithfully attend the convention sessions, spending just part of a single night roaming Downtown Disney. Other than that little venture, my Orlando theme park experience will be Holy Land. It will have to do.

I pay my ticket, still $29.99. And I get a "Shalom" and a "God Bless" from the clerk, a sign that this park wants to keep its own distinctive theme. I enter into the now familiar-looking Middle Eastern village, which I recall from my visit last year. The camels have been moved closer to the visiting throngs. The Florida humidity seems odd for these creatures, but they are certainly familiar with the hot sun.

We are told that the show begins at 9:30 a.m.,

set to begin next to the model of the Qumran Cave, Holy Land's version of where the Dead Sea Scrolls were found back in the 1940s. We are waiting in the desultory tourist air. Few of us know that we will be part of the show. A tall man in his 20s jostles through the crowd, his hands pushed ahead of him, as he makes his presence known. He is dressed in Middle Eastern garb and is supposed to be blind. He cries out for alms for the poor. He is, of course, an actor, and we are soon to witness another little Passion play, the kind that I remember vividly from last year.

In comes Jesus—he is more Tab Hunter than Jim Caviezel.

In comes Jesus through the crowd. He is less Semitic looking than last year's Jesus. He has the traditional beard and the long flowing hippie hair. Yet he is more Tab Hunter than Jim Caviezel.

This Jesus is friendly, approachable, spouting off parables with a smile and a glimmer in his eye. He is the kind of guy you wouldn't mind at a party, other than that he does tend towards the preachy. He heals a woman with a bleeding disorder and he heals the blind man who makes the distracting noise like a panhandler on the E-train.

High above the scene, two Jewish high priests

look down. They are ominous. And, as in the Gospels, they ask Jesus some trick questions about the Sabbath and obeying Roman authority, which he deflects—an easy task for the Son of God. Our audience this morning includes some two dozen young people from a day camp, and they are absorbed as Jesus holds a little lamb and tells them that he is the Good Shepherd.

A lot has happened in the evangelical world over the past year. After some effort and phone calls, I had a short conversation with Holy Land's founder. He was not too enthusiastic about talking to me. Later I find that the Holy Land concept has been burned in the press before. Author Timothy Beal derided the concept as "Christian edutainment" and complained about what he described as its saccharine character. I run across many articles written with a tone of a slight sneer about the entire project.

Mel Gibson's movie created an evangelical sensation, and the country has credited this group—or blamed it—for the re-election of George W. Bush. It is obvious that the Holy Land is trying to keep up. We enter the 9:45 a.m. "Theatre of Life" presentation where we are overwhelmed with the big picture of the history of the world in about 30 minutes. This is

Christian dogma taken out of the church and into the theme park, a facet of faith that evangelicals do so well. My little friend back in New York would be appalled, but I find myself impressed with this evangelical inclination to bring God into parts of American culture where he is usually quietly left behind.

The show is called "Seed of Promise," and we are told all about Adam and Eve—standing amid the usual strategically placed trees and bushes to hide their nakedness—complete with an omniscient, "God" narrator to explain the meaning of the Fall. Next comes Abraham about ready to sacrifice Isaac. If a Martian were to view this without context, he would obviously come to the conclusion that this particular Judeo-Christian God is no softie and is prone to capricious whimsy. In fact, he's got something of a mean streak.

Of course, this story of salvation ends with a meek and mild Jesus, walking the road to Emmaus, breaking bread with his disciples who do not recognize him in his resurrected form. That is a curiously strong Catholic Eucharistic image. It is a movie with glitz and passion, and one can easily understand that it is intended to appeal in particular to young people with its foreboding, sometimes violent images, and hints of sex. For the proverbial Martian not overly familiar with the scriptural themes, this could be powerful stuff.

Yet it's followed by an evangelical weakness. There's a preacher outside to explain it all to us. The images cannot be allowed just to speak for themselves. As he talks about awaiting the conversion of the Jews, I've had enough and drift off towards the air-conditioned comfort of a musical and cultural presentation.

This is where it gets interesting. It's at this point where the evangelical and the Catholic worlds intersect. Here is a presentation of Christian involvement in music and art, and of course it cannot be done without overt references to the Catholic world. And this show does so. We have Gregorian chant explained, as well as Michelangelo's Sistine Chapel fresco, and a warning that modern art lacks a coherent moral vision and reflects a disordered world. Our young and handsome guide walks us through these thousands of years of history with the assistance of singers and actors, some in period garb. All this has its culminating point, of course: it's American contemporary Christian rock, in which the lyrics, just as in nearly every evangelical church these days, are transposed on the screen as the entire auditorium of 1,000 or so clap to the beat.

It's a lot to take in. Evangelicals, of course, are known for exploring the big picture. Still, it's not bad. Its cultural and artistic milestones could be the focus of a semester in Christian cultural history at any challenging university. It is a sign to me that evangelicals are becoming more comfortable in exploring the culture and what it means, as well as history that extends beyond today or biblical times. The uncritical view of Christian rock, however, is befuddling. I find it hard to believe that Amy Grant is the culmination of Western religious culture.

I press on, wandering over to the gift shop to purchase postcards for those friends of mind who probably wouldn't be caught dead here in Holy Land. It's easy to ridicule what's here. I am conscious of being a kind of cultural snob delving into an exotic culture of the red states. So be it.

By the time I listen in on the Jerusalem panorama presentation, I've had a lot to absorb. But I strain to hear more. The presenter is a different one from last year's event—more preachy, more filled with jokes, and less scholarly. I get the sense he doesn't know as much about first-century life in Palestine as his counterpart I heard a year ago. He also drifts into another explanation of the end days, an evangelical obsession I have come to be impatient with, particularly its easy explanations of the complex world of Middle East politics and its tendency to be overly familiar with the mysteries of the vast future of the world.

As I sit and chomp on my Bedouin burger at the Holy Land cafeteria, I am struck that a serious religious scholar can look beyond the kitsch of Holy Land and see much of what both ails and inspires American Christian life today. If my thesis is correct, this is a spot which reflects American Christian religious culture, both evangelical and Catholic, in many ways merging into one stream, at other points remaining sharply divided.

Here is diversity. Again, the stereotype of the evangelical as exclusively Middle American and Caucasian doesn't hold. On my day at Holy Land, the buses come up filled with church groups. Out comes congregants of all ages speaking Haitian Creole and Latino Spanish. Some have come all the way from churches in Miami, hundreds of miles away.

From the beginning, I hear "Shalom" constantly uttered by staff. If there is any doctrinal point defined by evangelicals over the past two decades, it has been their obsession with things Jewish and Israeli. It is the evangelical world that encourages a strong pro-Israeli American foreign policy. Holy Land itself was founded by a Jewish convert to Christianity. Holy Land's pro-Jewish message, however, is mixed with another message: today's Jews are largely placeholders being readied for the return of Christ to the real Holy Land in all his glory. Not sure, if I were Jewish, this was something I would appreciate.

And, as has been the case for many sad centuries, Christian iconography with its more than a hint of anti-Semitism prevails here. Jesus has flowing gold highlights. His enemies are deeply Semitic looking and speak in harsh tones. Does this reflect the reality of the Gospel story or is it something deeper? I'm not ready to give a definitive answer, but the question still lingers.

The mainstreaming of evangelical life into American life continues in any case. Here is where the popularizing of many of the themes of more scholarly evangelical scholars is brought forth in the quintessential American entertainment format, the theme park. Here is reflected what I've read in articles and talked with scholars over the past year about developments in evangelical life.

Evangelicals today are struggling with their role in the history of Christianity. They are more willing to expand that history beyond the Reformation and the founding of American religious freedom. They are dealing with the Catholic influence on their own culture, with a twist, however. In traditional Catholic circles, the apex of Christian music is Gregorian chant; here, all music leads towards the formation of contemporary Christian rock, with its repetitive lyrics and bouncy beat that gets a crowd going.

Evangelicals are pioneers in bringing American pop culture and baptizing it into the Christian realm. They were the first—and largely, even today, the only—group that uses radio effectively. As far as religious groups go, they continue to dominate television and music formats today, as well as the religion and self-help aisles at the local chain bookstores. The history of Christianity conveyed at Orlando's Holy Land involves spreading the gospel through all media forms, including movies. The spectre of Mel Gibson's *Passion* is echoed here. Modern American religion, particularly its evangelical version with its ongoing Catholic influences, is here on display for anyone to see. As long as, of course, they are willing to pony up the $29.99.

9

Meshing two worlds

While attending the Catholic press convention in May 2005, I bring up the theme of this book with some of the editors who come from the heart of the Bible Belt. They cope with spreading the Catholic version of Christianity in places where evangelicalism reigns supreme, such as central Texas and rural Kentucky.

"You should come down where we are," said one Texas editor, describing his own journey from evangelical Presbyterianism, to the Catholic charismatic movement, into full communion with the Church. There was a tone indicating that perhaps a northeasterner who hasn't really lived near the Bible Belt culture would have difficulty comprehending it.

And to a certain extent, he's right. I am New York born and bred, although leavened by time in such outposts as Ohio, Indiana, and Michigan. I can remember one summer as a college youth on a church mission to rural Kentucky, and the one early evening I spent listening to a hot-headed preacher in a small-frame church. I don't remember what he said, but I do remember the intensity with which he said it, an alien world to those immersed into the more laid-back world of northeastern American Catholicism.

But the fact that the evangelical world has reached into my life—albeit in the small ways recounted in this short volume—is an indication that something is happening out there that's worth paying attention to. When the Bible Belt begins wrapping itself around old-time Catholics like those who run in my circle, it's evident that evangelicalism has begun to break out of its spiritual ghetto.

Part of it, of course, is due to media coverage. Once a movement that existed almost solely in its insular world—until the occasional sex or money scandal caused periodic public uproars—after the election of 2004 the elite media began playing catch-up with a phenomena it barely knew existed before.

Two summers ago, I was part of a religion and journalism class at Northwestern University. As I described earlier in this book, our graduate class roamed the Chicago area, exploring American religious diversity, visiting everyone from Sikhs and Scientologists to Sephardic Jews, as well as run-of-the-mill Catholics and Protestants.

My classmates—half of us were professional religion writers, the other half Northwestern grad students—talked frequently about how we wished our experience could be transported into America's newsrooms. We envisioned a day when media might actually take religion seriously.

Our sentiments were, of course, borne out of self-interest. As a group, we were paid, or wanted to be paid, for reporting on the world of the soul. But we also were filled with idealistic notions that more coverage of religion would mean greater understanding and insight into the wide gamut of faith expression we experienced that summer in Chicago.

We got what we wished for. Religion coverage

has skyrocketed. But maybe we should have been more careful about what we wished for. Apparently spurred on by the results of the 2004 election, coverage of faith has increased in quantity. At the same time, it has focused narrowly on developments within the Christian Right. To be Christian in America, the drumbeat of media coverage seems to indicate, is to be a rural conservative evangelical or a Catholic who cheers the conservative direction of the new pope. Christianity is routinely equated with Republican party affiliation. To be Christian is to be obsessed with gay marriage and the role of public policy on sexual issues generally.

Those who don't fit in, yet still hold to the Christian label, are barely recognized. I checked out a local library to search for how many articles on "Christian conservatives" were counted by a popular search engine over a month in the spring of 2005. The answer was well over 1,000. The number of articles on "Christian liberals": zero. Another search engine, this one focused on major newspapers, offered a more balanced picture: 21 articles were on the theme of liberal Christians, while the conservatives got 257.˙

It's clear that evangelical conservatism is what makes the headlines these days. The *Columbia Jour-*

nalism Review recently reported on the growth of evangelical Christian news gathering, resulting in the Terri Schiavo story becoming the political steamroller it became. Christian moralists opposed to the heavy hand of government intervention in this case were largely absent from coverage, which was framed in a Christian vs. secular framework. The *Los Angeles Times* reported on faith in the workplace, of course focused on how evangelicals are proselytizing amid the cubicles. In Kansas, we hear about Christians concerned about stopping or downplaying the teaching of evolution.

So why this sudden interest in conservative evangelical Christians? Their numbers, according to the best studies, have not spiked over the past few years. It is clear, however, that in the aftermath of the election media elites on the two coasts suddenly discovered they were out of touch with middle American religious people. Panic seems to have set in. For example: The internal *New York Times* report on its newsgathering notes that its coverage of gay marriage has suffered from an inability to recognize the deeply felt religious revulsion to the idea, which its reporters have tended to frame only in terms of human rights. You would think their reporters would occasionally venture into New Jersey and discover this self-evident truth for themselves.

There's also the political angle. Evangelical Christians are said to be a new political force, even though their numbers and activism have not increased considerably over the past few years. What's different is that they are now recognized as political players, a paradigm that reporters are accustomed to covering.

Yet that focus is a lingering insult to evangelicals. Anyone who even occasionally visits an evangelical church knows that politics

> You would think New York Times reporters would occasionally venture into New Jersey and discover this self-evident truth for themselves.

has little to do with the appeal of that movement. Much media attention focuses on old-time political players such as the Rev. Pat Robertson. However, he's old school. In a poll of evangelicals taken last year, the Rev. Robertson was far below the late Pope John Paul II among the list of admired religious leaders.

The new face of evangelicalism is more seen in the youthful countenance of preachers such as Rev. Joel Osteen of Houston, whose national telecasts barely touch on the Scriptures, much less politics. His congregation has taken over an old basketball arena to accommodate the 30,000 who regularly attend Sunday services. Rev. Osteen is much more the self-help guru than political power player. His message is a simple one, based on being nice to your family and friends—a positive and hardly threatening view. The so-called megachurches, such as Willow Creek in the outer Chicago suburbs, are largely gathering places for like-minded conservative people seeking religious community and support. They are not political club-houses. The best coverage reflects this reality; the worst just continues to see religious life in America in hackneyed left/right terms.

What is obvious is that the small slice of Christians who embrace the Far Right are well organized and, while complaining that they are persecuted, gladly seek out coverage. It's those squeaky wheels who are creating the noise, while the rest of religious Christian America goes about its business, far removed from the media spotlight. The resulting media coverage has made the phrase "Christian conservative" into a popular tautology, to the regret of those of us who think that the Gospels offer more guidance on forgiving your enemies than on legislative fili-busters (or how to eliminate them).

So beyond the media coverage, what are Catholics to do? Can we co-exist with our evangelical neighbors? Are we doomed to a future in which the evangelical brand of Christianity will become dominant, and the Catholic liturgical vision will have to take a backseat?

Evangelicals might well have similar questions about their Catholic neighbors. But it's hard for this author to address them. It might well be worthwhile for an evangelical to further explore what impact Catholicism has on evangelical Protestantism in the U.S.

What strikes me about the Catholic responses to evangelicals is how quiet they have been, at least till now. Pope Benedict XVI has issued dire warnings about secular relativists, to some great publicity, yet has generated little response to his criticism of various "sects" active in Latin America. He couldn't have been happy when more than a million evangelicals marched publicly in Brazil just a month after his election in what is the world's most populous Catholic country.

Here in Holy Land U.S.A,. it's obvious that church officials need to take evangelicalism seriously. One small step would help. Catholic pastors need to spend at least one Sunday a year at a local evangelical church, whether a Spanish Pentecostal congregation in our large cities or a megachurch in a sprawling exurb.

What would they find? For one thing, they would need to get over the snob appeal directed against evangelicals throughout the culture. Highly educated people—and priests are among them—usually have a low opinion of evangelicals. It seems to me that much ecumenical progress is made with main-line Protestants and Catholic clergy largely because it is a more pleasant social conversation. It's easier to share lunch where there's general cultural affinity.

Evangelicals are another matter. Catholic visitors to evangelical churches would discover the value of dynamic preaching in a worship service. It's hard to believe that the generally low level of preaching in Catholic churches could continue if priests knew the quality of the delivery—if not the material—that is delivered up the block or down the road.

Business Week reports that evangelicals have successfully adapted to American business models. Catholicism, it reports, continues to be popular yet its decline in church population is hidden by an influx of Catholic immigrant groups in recent years that have tended to prop up its market share.

Evangelicals, largely unencumbered by a top-down management style, are better able to respond to needs. The megachurches and their various small groups illustrate how flexible their model of ministry can be. Many preachers, such as the Rev. Osteen of Houston, have been able to tap into a growing market for the "prosperity gospel," in which Jesus rewards those who use their talents most effectively. It's horrible theology, but there is obviously a niche for such an appeal in a culture that worships upward mobility as much as this one does.

Catholic visitors to evangelical churches would also find out something new as well. They will discover that politics is rarely discussed in such precincts. The political/evangelical link is largely something blown up by reporters seeking a political angle. They do so because it is a paradigm—Democrats vs. Republicans, conservatives vs. liberals—that they are comfortable in engaging. The world of the spiritual and Scripture is another realm indeed.

I'm a regular churchgoer, both Catholic and, for the purposes of this book, evangelical as well. In a time when politics was at its hottest—the run-up and immediate aftermath to the 2004 election—I never heard a word preached about politics in either venue.

The only thing that came close was an injunction from an evangelical pastor at a Long Island church to support our troops in Iraq, a plea that came across more as praise for twenty-first-century Christian crusaders than as a disinterested hope for peace and an end to casualties. Maybe in other parts of the country the political angle is common, but in Florida and the Northeast, the two regions I visited regularly and live in, it rarely rears its ugly partisan head.

Evangelicals may have a fire-and-brimstone reputation, but the reality is more Oprah. Instead of raining down God's wrath, evangelical preachers are more likely to embrace American therapeutic culture. Family relationships and dysfunctions take a central role. How to heal marriages is more often talked about than God's wrath. Megachurches are built around common communities. Often those groups focus on healing personal issues, much like Oprah Winfrey does on her daily television show, providing homespun advice for problems usually associated with marriage and family life.

Don't know how scriptural that approach is—if one reads the New Testament, Jesus has if anything a kind of detached near-disdain for the particularities of family life, and St. Paul certainly believes that one's relationship with God, not marriage or family life, is priority number one. Yet it is comforting to know that, despite media reports to the contrary, therapeutic support beats out rabid right-wing politics in so many evangelical churches. The loneliness and isolation of the transient family living out in wider rims of American metropolitan areas is a social crisis that evangelical churches have been most successful in recognizing and addressing.

That is to their credit. All this is happening, however, largely under the radar screen of Catholics, evangelicals' largest fellow pilgrims on the Christian path. Outside of a serious effort to address evangelicals' outreach to Latino immigrants, Catholics are largely oblivious to the impact evangelicals are having on the wider culture, even as the church slowly adapts Scripture study, support groups and other pastoral practices into the Catholic parish mix.

There are some Catholic leaders, however, who recognize the evangelical impact. One is Jesuit Father Manuel Flores, a professor at the Loyola School of Theology in Quezon City, the Philippines. He came over to Fuller Theological Seminary in California, one of the world's largest evangelical seminaries, to discover how successful evangelical churches grow both in the U.S. and in his historically Catholic country of the Philippines.

In an interview with the Jesuit magazine *America* in 2004, Father Flores said he came away from his studies at Fuller with the conclusion that what sets evangelicals apart is not their theology but their method. "They use what works," he says. Because they are largely unencumbered by a top-down leadership struggle, they are able to explore, build small communities, and incorporate methods that reach people and discard those that don't. In that way, they mimic American corporate marketing. Other traditions, particularly Roman Catholicism, are more tied down, not only in essentials, such as the liturgy, but also in non-essentials. How many moribund Catholic parish organizations continue to survive, many with aging and dwindling memberships, while outreach to groups such as young adults goes untended? How often do Catholic parishes tend to the niches of regular churchgoers—such as education of young children and the growing demands of a senior citizen population—and fail to take note of who isn't coming to Mass,

> It may be that what sets evangelicals apart is not their theology but their method.

particularly young adults and teens? That is a failure any pastor of a thriving evangelical church would address first, not last.

Still, if the emergence of evangelicals threatens to provide an erroneous conclusion for Catholic church leaders, it would be this one: Evangelicals succeed because they offer a strong message of moral chastisement to a corrupt world. This is the kind of conclusion drawn by church leaders who mingle with evangelical leaders at political rallies and have little idea what happens inside those giant boxes of worship built on recovered farmland all over the country.

That image of evangelicalism—the fiery preacher denouncing moral ills—is familiar to all, evangelical and non-evangelical. But what's more important is the quiet world of evangelical congregations, particularly the megachurch, built on social support and not moral chastisement.

It is the kind of false conclusion comfortable with church leaders who believe stringent denominational lines and arcane theological debates over justification and other issues matter greatly to most people in the pews. They don't.

Megachurches thrive largely on the outer rims of great cities, places where there is transient life and where established churches have been slow to move into. They offer a warm, socializing institution amidst the box stores and housing developments that mar the landscape. If they get the comforting words of Scripture in the bargain, so be it. But it's hard to believe that a Catholic Church that is perceived as more rigid on sexuality issues—such as gay rights and particularly divorce and remarriage—would be a more attractive institution to such people. Evangelical congregations are often filled, according to anecdotal evidence one priest told me, by fallen-away Catholics who are remarried and divorced, who have a difficult time navigating the Church's strict interpretation of the words of Jesus on that subject.

Whatever Catholics bring away from the evangelical phenomenon, both groups will continue to draw from each other. After all, in a country where religion, and in particular Christianity, exerts itself more and more, it is those two groups that will be seen as the keepers of the tradition. It is a huge responsibility, building this Holy Land. And it will take more than $29.99 and an afternoon in the hot Florida sun to see how this reality gets lived out.

10

Afterword: Bridging the Simpson/Flanders divide

He's the owner of the Springfield Leftorium, the mall store selling left-handed products. Although 60 years old, he looks young and buff for his age, and, as a widowed father, is particularly devoted to his young sons, Rod and Todd. Some say his constant references to everything as "okily dokily" is annoying, others claim it's a charming eccentricity.

But beyond these traits, Ned Flanders is best known for being perhaps the nation's most widely recognized evangelical, as every week (and through the magic of reruns, daily), he drives Homer Simpson into mad rages in response to Ned's good nature and strong Christian faith.

Ned is, literally and figuratively, a cartoon character, a kind of stereotype of evangelicals. Still, his persona is embraced by clubs of young college campus evangelicals in the United States and evangelical Christians in Britain who have gathered together in mini-festivals in his honor. His public fans even include Rowan Williams, the Archbishop of Canterbury.

As American evangelicals assert themselves in the public square—they have been credited (or blamed) for exerting political control over the executive and legislative branches of the federal government—the genial, apolitical Ned has become someone nearly everyone can identify. The question for those of us who are not evangelicals is—how do we respond to the Flanders in our midst, whether across the backyard fence or in the workplace?

> How do we respond to the Flanders in our midst, whether across the backyard fence or in the workplace?

Knowledgeable Catholics, often a target for zealous evangelicals who frequently see the Church's tradition as overly stuffy, non-scriptural, and not conversion-oriented, find the fuming Homer Simpson approach doesn't work very well.

Mary Pat Campbell of Queens, New York, says knowledge about one's own Catholic faith helps. She finds it necessary to have some knowledge of old Reformation arguments. "We don't still sell indulgences," she says, pointing out an old canard often raised by zealous evangelical proselytizers.

Evangelicals often point to Scripture as the basis for their beliefs, arguing that Catholic tradition has muddied the waters of pure Christian doctrine. But Campbell points out that the end of John's Gospel says that not everything pertinent to matters of salvation are contained in the Bible. And, when she encounters a strong fundamentalist—one who argues that everything in Scripture is literally true—she notes that even Jesus spoke in the figurative language of parables.

A lawyer from Ohio, who wants to remain anonymous to maintain family peace, has had faith encounters with an evangelical brother-in-law. It hasn't always been an easygoing relationship.

"It comes across as a bit of an affront to hear that someone is praying that you will find Christ," he says, noting that the rest of his Catholic family will not discuss religion with his brother-in-law, who is quick to hand out tracts and argue that the Church fosters idol worship in its devotion to Mary and the saints. The attorney has taken their religious argument away from the family get-together and put it online. The end result: a respectful impasse, the attorney believing that the friendly Jesus promoted by most evangelicals is largely uninspiring and his brother-in-law believing that salvation cannot be found in the Catholic Church.

These day-to-day encounters in the United States reflect a universal concern. The Catholic Church continues a worldwide struggle with evangelicals, tempered in some cases with alliances on cultural issues such as sexual morality and abortion. The most zealous among them continue to annoy those of us more comfortably ensconced in a secular culture.

One such person is Rick Zimmer of Anchorage, Alaska (full disclosure: Rick is a cousin of mine), a commercial airline pilot who finds that his workplace time includes religion discussions instigated by co-workers who are evangelical in outlook.

Alaska, once known for a secularized individual-ism, has undergone an evangelical surge in recent years. Zimmer noted that a fellow pilot once felt compelled to shout from the tarmac to his opened window on his plane, "Are you a believer?" Zimmer, raised a Catholic, answered "Unitarian," only to be met with a quizzical look.

"I frequently fly with guys who pull out their Bibles and spend their free hours highlighting the significant passages with yellow highlighters," he says.

Zimmer occasionally enjoys a good religion argument. He will discuss the merits of the thought of Joseph Campbell, the late philosopher who analyzed religious and cultural mythology. All in all, he's gained respect for evangelical faith, although he sometimes wonders if that same respect is accorded his beliefs.

"I've been to some of their services and I can see the attraction if a pep rally is the sort of thing you're looking for—and it made me realize that my liberal church has serious competition with a message that is not being received," he says.

"I've met people who were Christian that just radiated happiness and contentment—even I have been impressed. In truth, I don't want to win my arguments with those guys and unmoor them from the rock they have based their life on. I would feel terrible. I really don't care what they believe, but I find their certainty and those with intolerance of other faiths to be annoying and dangerous, and I cannot understand it," he says.

Those with a more devout Catholic background find that aggressive evangelicals can cause them to explore their own faith more deeply.

"I definitely like them," notes Rich Leonardi, a writer from Cincinnati, Ohio. "As opposed to many if not most Catholics, evangelicals keep Christ central to their family lives. I recall one evangelical co-worker telling me how much he and his young son enjoyed spending Christmas Eve participating in a 'Meals on Wheels' program his community sponsored. He was clearly witnessing but also clearly happy to share his story."

Catholics who encounter evangelicals need to have more than a passing familiarity with the Bible, says Leonardi. They also should not be afraid to be publicly pious. At first many evangelical acquaintances are dismissive when they discover he is a Catholic, "but once they learn that at least a few of these ritualistic Catholics actually read the Bible and

can say the word 'Jesus' without looking embar-
rassed, they give the matter additional considera-
tion," he says.

Others prefer the more combative Homer
Simpson-type approach.

Larry, a Queens, New York electrician, regularly
encounters a proselytizing evangelical on his job.
Larry, a self-described "very reformed" Jew married
to a Catholic, has allied with his Jewish and Catholic
co-workers to create a combative religiously charged
atmosphere. The proselytizing evangelical has created
resentment at the worksite.

According to his evangelical co-worker,
"Catholic people aren't quite religious enough. And
Jews won't even have a chance to get to heaven," says
Larry, who notes that he and his fellows will deliber-
ately rile up their evangelical co-worker for early
morning coffee amusement.

"We occasionally make believe to get him all intense," he says, noting that they ask him loaded theological questions such as why God allows deadly
hurricanes to occur. "But like toothpaste out of the
tube, you can't shut him up," says Larry.

Few Catholic clergy have as much experience
in dealing with evangelicals as Glenmary Father

John Rausch, coordinator of the Peace and Justice
Office for the Diocese of Lexington, Kentucky.
Rausch is a member of a community devoted to
Catholic ministry in the Bible Belt. He believes
there is a third way between downgrading evangelical beliefs and high-toned theological discussions
with them.

Many Catholics, he says, need to get used to
evangelical language and tone. Common phrases,
such as "Praise God," are regularly recited by evangelicals, and they frequently ask, "Are you saved?"
with the world easily divided between those who can
say yes to that question and everyone else.

When asked if he is saved, Father Rausch responds with something like this: "We Catholics really
don't use that phrase. We feel that we constantly
grow in our devotion to God. For us conversion is a
step, rather than a one-time moment."

His advice to Catholics, and others, dealing with
evangelicals is something he learned from tennis:
"Never slug with a slugger." In other words, there is
little use in getting involved in large theological discussions, particularly those based on rote recitations
of biblical passages. The Catholic tradition, which
combines faith in the Scriptures, tradition and human

reason, is at variance with a zealous evangelical view that relies on Scripture alone, he says.

When it comes to arguing scriptural "proof texts," says Rausch, "Catholics will be at a loss." But that doesn't mean that Catholics and evangelicals can't talk and work together, he emphasizes.

Evangelical leaders such as Jim Wallis and Rick Warren are now rediscovering that tradition's social gospel, galvanizing the movement to become concerned about poverty in America and overseas. There is a growing consensus among Christians of all stripes, says Father Rausch, that the Gospels clearly indicate that Jesus stood with the poor and that is the obligation of all his followers. Evangelicals and Catholics, he says, can find common ground through "works of charity and the works of justice."

Yet, many don't have a lot of time to devote to ecumenical social action projects. If there is a Ned Flanders lurking behind the backyard fence or in the next office cubicle, it can still be awkward.

Catholics sympathetic to evangelical devotion to the Scriptures and the seriousness with which many of them take their Christianity, point out that perhaps Ned Flanders—and his evangelical friends—are not so bad after all.

"That dear old Ned is being portrayed here as some kind of villain is terribly unfair to him. His bubbly optimism and consistent Christian forgiveness makes him one of the most admirable characters on television. Hasn't he suffered enough, with the tragic death of his wife, and the numerous indignities that Homer and his son have visited upon him?" says *Simpsons* fan Father Brian Stanley, pastor of St. Charles Church in Coldwater, Michigan.

Some devout Catholics argue that it's the widespread secularism, not Ned Flanders, that provides the greatest challenges to faith-loving people. Noted one California Catholic: "Maybe it's because I'm out in Los Angeles and to come across an openly committed Christian is an anomaly itself—not saying there aren't many good Christians out here, just you tend to come across many more bitter, angry, secularists. All the evangelicals I've met out here realize there are many good Catholics and follow Christ's saying 'If they're not against us, they're for us.'"

185

Still, there are some who, like Homer, prefer their religion in tidy one-hour Sunday segments and are wary of someone who brings Jesus to the public square. In one episode, when Ned brings his neighbor some doughnuts from the church, Homer responds testily: "It's always gotta be about church with you, doesn't it? Flanders, for the last time, I am not interested in your evangelical doughnuts." It is perhaps the only time in the history of the Simpsons that Homer has turned down his favorite food.

Perhaps it is an indication that the world could use an attitude adjustment on both sides of the Homer/Flanders divide. Evangelicals could learn to appreciate the value of tolerance and pluralism, while the rest of us could grow in appreciation of a segment of our society who take Christianity seriously. It wouldn't kill anyone to partake in an occasional evangelical doughnut—taken, of course, in moderation.